Student Portfolios
A Collection of Articles

Edited by
Robin Fogarty

IRI/Skylight Training and Publishing, Inc.
Palatine, Illinois

Student Portfolios: A Collection of Articles
First Printing

Published by IRI/Skylight Training and Publishing, Inc.
200 E. Wood Street, Suite 274
Palatine, Illinois 60067
800-348-4474 or 847-991-6300
FAX 847-991-6420
irisky@xnet.com
http://www.business1.com/iri_sky/

Creative Director: Robin Fogarty
Managing Editor: Julia Noblitt
Editors: Amy Wolgemuth, Troy Slocum
Proofreader: Sabine Vorkoeper
Type Compositor: Donna Ramirez
Formatter: Donna Ramirez
Illustration and Cover Design: David Stockman
Book Designer: Bruce Leckie
Production Supervisor: Bob Crump

Printed in the United States of America.
ISBN 0-57517-011-6

Library of Congress Catalog Card Number: 95-81913

1683-1-96 V
Item number 1422

ontents

Student Portfolios
A Collection of Articles

Learning preserves the errors of the past, as well as its wisdom.—Alfred North Whitehead

A portable case for holding papers, drawings" is the unassuming definition given to the word *portfolio* in the American Heritage Dictionary. It is this idea of "a case that holds the papers and drawings" that encapsulates the current use of a student portfolio in the learner-centered classroom of the 1990s. Of course, the actual development and use of the student portfolio in today's kindergarten to college classrooms encompasses much more—a cadre of philosophical, organizational, and implementational considerations.

Questions that accompany this idea range from the most basic and practical questions—"What are portfolios, really?" "How do we do them?" "Who does them?" "Where do we store them?"—to the more philosophical questions of "Why should we do them?" and "What do they provide that traditional assessments don't already provide?" In addition, procedural questions arise, including "How are they used?" "What weight do they carry in terms of the overall assessment of the student?" and "Do portfolios replace all other methods of assessment?"

In fact, the idea of student portfolios, while simple in its initial concept, may quite possibly be more like the proverbial Pandora's box than the aforementioned "portable case." For the idea of student portfolios does indeed create a boxful of decisions that must be made, as indicated by the plethora of questions suggested above.

With these concerns voiced clearly at the outset, the motive behind *Student Portfolios: A Collection of Articles* begins to come into focus. This collection of pertinent articles, from leading voices in the field, is provided as a primer to the idea of exploring, deciding to use, and actually using student portfolios in the classroom. All written within the past few years, the essays gathered here are organized into three distinct groupings that target the areas of choosing, using, and perusing portfolios.

Section 1: The Vision: Choosing Portfolios focuses on the initial concerns that accompany the exploration of the student portfolio as a viable assessment tool. The articles in this section provide the "big picture" about student portfolios, giving readers the opportunity to survey the concept of portfolio assessment as a bridge from traditional assessment to more authentic measures, as well as to look at portfolios as a new instrument in the changing paradigm of schooling created by the constructivist philosophy of learning.

Section 2: The Mission: Using Portfolios highlights the practical concerns of implementing portfolios in the classroom, and the many and varied aspects of the actual implementation process. Essays in this section address the issues of purpose, content, value, assessment of work samples in portfolios, and the role of electronic portfolios. The authors approach questions of what we really care about in portfolio use, how to make them user friendly, the actual contents of portfolios, ways to evaluate through student work samples, and how technology enhances our use of portfolios.

Section 3: The Message: Perusing Portfolios targets the reflective sharing of the portfolio in the total assessment process. In this final collection of writings, the authors discuss the self-assessment element of portfolios, the role of student-led parent conferences as an enhancement to portfolio use, questions parents have regarding portfolios and portfolio conferences, and the serendipitous benefit of portfolios in terms of reflections for staff as well as for students.

In concluding these introductory remarks, it seems prudent to note one perhaps not-so-obvious truth about the use of student portfolios. The opening definition of portfolios as "a portable case for holding papers," chosen for its simplicity in presenting a complex idea, may also be a bit misleading. For the authenticity of portfolio assessment rests in the process itself: collecting work samples over time, periodically selecting key pieces for final inclusion in the portfolio, reflecting on the meaning of each artifact, and eventually showcasing the portfolio for peers, parents, and teachers. In fact, it is this continual process of portfolio development and the sharing with an audience that is alluded to in the term "processfolio," often used by Howard Gardner (see *Multiple Intelligences: The Theory into Practice*, 1993). As stated so eloquently by Robert Louis Stevenson, "To travel hopefully is a better thing than to arrive." It is the reflective journey and the anticipation of an audience that provides the motivation for student involvement. And it is the striving for perfection that drives the student to select and reflect with care, judgment, and insight. In sum, it is the process *in total* that undergirds the value of portfolio assessments.

The Vision: Choosing Portfolios

Growth is the only evidence of life.—John Henry Newman

To open this collection, a selection of four articles sets the stage for realizing the vision of portfolio assessment in the overall evaluation scheme. While traditional assessments provide demographic data through the use of grades and rankings, portfolio assessments and performance-based assessments add new dimensions to the picture of student progress. More specifically, portfolios foster continual, ongoing reflection by the student and the teacher on the growth and development of the student, while performance-based assessments promote relevance and transfer of learning by requiring performance of a relevant task. The call for portfolio assessments is clear—schools are choosing portfolios as valid, reliable, and reflective assessment tools.

In the opening article, Linda Darling-Hammond sets the stage for "choosing portfolios" by suggesting that when assessment allows students to achieve challenging goals in authentic ways, it also helps create confident learners. In a very real sense, the instruction becomes the assessment and the assessment becomes the instruction. This approach precludes the age-old idea of the teacher as the giver of knowledge and the giver of grades;

instead, the responsibility for learning is shared by the student and the teacher. Contrasting the historical approach to testing with the growing consensus among today's educators that change is needed, the article supplies a vision of a more complete picture of human potential than that provided by traditional assessments alone.

In the second article, Brenda S. Engel presents the new paradigm in education that emphasizes meaning as the energizing force. Constructivism is now guiding many educational decisions, which means this new paradigm is impacting evaluation and assessment as well as curriculum and instruction. The author talks about the new responsibilities for teachers as these new assessments are initiated. In addition, the power of student portfolios is revealed through authentic student samples. The students' learning is evident as efforts to construct meaning are voiced in portfolio artifacts.

Yet another piece is included to provide that vision of portfolios as a necessary and welcome tool in the constructivist paradigm. F. Leon Paulson and Pearl R. Paulson, a well-respected duo in the field, present a full and comprehensive assessment of portfolios through what they call the "cognitive model for assessing portfolios." Tracking two projects involving multidimensional approaches, they compare the efforts, defining one as a positivist paradigm and the other as a constructivist paradigm. One project looks at the end results in the portfolio, while the other looks at the process of the portfolio use. They conclude that testing is top down and that portfolios are bottom up; therefore, portfolios seem better suited to the constructivist model, which stresses making meaning, than to the positivist approach, which stresses psychometric aggregations.

Finally, Susan Black's reader-friendly article surveys some of the inherent problems that accompany the use of portfolio assessment as an alternative to traditional assessment. Although the author makes the point that the decision to use portfolios is the easiest part, the information presented here actually serves as critical data for helping the reader to decide whether or not to use portfolios. For, as in making any decision of worth, the decision makers must know the pros and the cons of the issues at hand. Black skillfully presents the spectrum of pluses and minuses that surround portfolio use. In the final analysis, the author provides a needed caution: Time must be invested in teachers *before* they begin portfolios and support must be there *after* they've started.

Setting Standards for Students: The Case for Authentic Assessment

by Linda Darling-Hammond

As students prepare for graduation at Central Park East Secondary School (CPESS), a high school of 450 students in an East Harlem neighborhood in New York City, they do not worry about assembling Carnegie Units, nor do they cram for multiple-choice Regents examinations as do many other students in high schools around New York. Instead, they work intensively during their one to three years in the CPESS Senior Institute preparing a portfolio of their work that will reveal their competence and performance in 14 curricular areas, ranging from science and technology to ethics and social issues, from school and community service to mathematics, literature, and history.

This portfolio will be evaluated by a graduation committee composed of teachers from different subjects and grade levels, an outside examiner, and a student peer. The committee members will examine all the entries and hear the students' oral "defense" of their work as they determine when each student is ready to graduate.

Part of the growing movement to establish means for more authentic assessment of student learning, CPESS is developing ways to focus students' energies on challenging performance-oriented tasks that require analysis, integration of knowledge, and invention as well as highly developed written and oral expression rather than merely recall and recognition of facts.

From *NASSP Bulletin*, vol. 77, no. 556, November 1993, pp. 18–26. © 1993 by the National Association of Secondary School Principals. Reprinted with permission.

Students develop a project that demonstrates their knowledge of scientific methodology, for example, by using it in a particular field. They engage ethical and social issues by participating in a debate, writing an op-ed article, or analyzing a film or novel that raises important moral issues.

> Increasingly, local schools, districts, and states are experimenting with . . . alternatives to standardized testing.

In each case, they must demonstrate their ability to see multiple viewpoints, weigh conflicting claims, and defend their views with credible evidence. Literary essays and historical analyses, along with documentation and evaluation of their internship experiences, add to the wealth of evidence students' accumulate about their attainment of valued school—and societal—goals.

Increasingly, local schools, districts, and states are experimenting with these methods and other alternatives to standardized testing for assessing student learning and performance. Much like the kinds of assessments that prevail in most other countries around the world—where multiple-choice testing is much less common—these approaches include essay examinations, research projects, scientific experiments, oral exhibitions, and performances in such areas as debating and the arts.

They also include portfolios of students' work in various subject areas, along with individual and group projects requiring analysis, investigation, experimentation, cooperation, and written, oral, or graphic presentation of findings. Often, the assessment occasion requires students to respond to questions from classmates or from external examiners, thus helping them learn to think through and defend their views, while allowing their teachers to hear and understand their thinking (Coalition of Essential Schools, 1990; Archbald and Newmann, 1988).

WHY ALTERNATIVE ASSESSMENT?
One of the reasons for these efforts to develop alternative forms of assessment is a growing consensus among educators, researchers, and policymakers that current U.S. tests do not tap many of the skills and abilities that students need to develop in order to be successful in later life and schooling. These concerns

are partly due to the limits of widely used U.S. testing methods, described more fully below. The concerns are also related to the increasing demands for a kind of education that encourages students to do more than memorize information and use it to solve tidy problems—an education that prepares students to frame problems, find information, evaluate alternatives, create ideas and products, and invent new answers to messy dilemmas.

The capacities required of students today are more demanding than those required in the past. A growing number of jobs in our information economy require highly developed intellectual skills and technological training. Even "low skill" jobs require technical training and flexibility. In addition, most industries are restructuring the way they organize work so that cooperative planning and problem solving are the "basic skills" that have replaced following simple directions on an assembly line.

The capacities required of students today are more demanding than those required in the past.

Citizens must be able to access resources and perform complicated tasks at high levels of literacy to survive in today's world. Workers must anticipate changing occupations several times over the course of a lifetime, adapting to everchanging technologies and job demands, and inventing solutions to productivity problems rather than relying on a manager to tell them what to do (Hudson Institute, 1987; Drucker, 1986).

These kinds of skills and abilities are not based on the kinds of thinking and performance that are evaluated in most U.S. testing programs. Because of the way widely used multiple-choice, norm-referenced tests are constructed, they exclude a great many kinds of knowledge and types of performance we expect from students, placing testtakers in a passive, reactive role, rather than one that engages their capacities to structure tasks, produce ideas, and solve problems (National Research Council, 1982). Current research on human learning and performance has suggested that many currently used tests fail to measure students' higher order cognitive abilities or to support their capacities to perform real-world tasks (Resnick, 1987; Sternberg, 1985).

CONCERNS ABOUT CURRENT TESTING POLICIES

These shortcomings were less problematic when the tests were used as only one of many kinds of information about student learning, and when they were not directly tied to decisions about students and programs. However, as test scores have been increasingly used to make important educational decisions, their flaws have become more damaging.

> Classwork oriented toward recognizing the answers to multiple-choice questions does not heighten students' proficiency in areas that are not tested.

As schools have begun to "teach to the tests," the scores have become ever poorer assessments of students' overall abilities, because classwork oriented toward recognizing the answers to multiple-choice questions does not heighten students' proficiency in areas that are not tested, such as analysis, complex problem solving, and written and oral expression (Koretz, 1988; Haney and Madaus, 1986; Darling-Hammond and Wise, 1985).

Because teachers must emphasize those things that tests measure, current approaches to testing often limit the kinds of teaching and learning opportunities provided in classrooms.

The results of this phenomenon can be seen in U.S. students' performance. Since about 1970, when standardized tests began to be used for a wider variety of accountability purposes, basic skills test scores have been increasing slightly, while assessments of higher order thinking skills have declined in virtually all subject areas. Officials of the National Assessment of Educational Progress, the National Research Council, and the National Councils of Teachers of English and Mathematics, among others, have all attributed this decline in higher order thinking and performance to schools' emphasis on tests of basic skills. They argue that not only are the test scores inadequate measures of students' performance abilities, but also that the uses of the tests have corrupted teaching practices.

As the National Assessment of Educational Progress found: "Only 5 to 10 percent of (high school) students can move beyond initial readings of a test; most seem genuinely puzzled at requests to explain or defend their points of view." The NAEP assessors explained that current methods of teaching and testing reading require short responses and lower level cognitive thinking, resulting in "an emphasis on shallow and superficial opinions at the expense of reasoned and disciplined thought . . . , (thus) it is not surprising that students fail to develop more comprehensive thinking and analytic skills" (NAEP, 1981).

A more recent NAEP report summarized the status of high school students' performance as follows:

> Sixty-one percent of the 17-year-old students could not read or understand relatively complicated material, such as that typically presented at the high school level. Nearly one-half appear to have limited mathematics skills and abilities that go little beyond adding, subtracting, and multiplying with whole numbers. More than one-half could not evaluate the procedures or results of a scientific study, and few included enough information in their written pieces to communicate their ideas effectively. Additionally, assessment results in other curriculum areas indicate that high school juniors have little sense of historical chronology, have not read much literature, and tend to be unfamiliar with the uses and potential applications of computers (LaPointe, et al., 1989, p. 26).

International comparisons of student performance in mathematics and science tell a similar story. U.S. students score at about the median of other countries at fifth grade, dip below the average by eighth grade, and consistently score near the bottom by twelfth grade, especially on tasks requiring higher order thinking and problem solving.

An international mathematics study found that, in line with U.S. testing demands, instruction in the United States is dominated by textbooks and lectures, followed by individual seatwork, with little use of other resources such as computers, calculators, or manipulatives.

The researchers concluded that these "strategies geared to rote learning" represent:

> . . . a view that learning for most students should be passive—teachers transmit knowledge to students who receive it and remember it mostly in the form in which it was transmitted. . . . In the light of this, it is hardly surprising that the achievement test items on which U.S. students most often showed relatively greater growth were those most suited to performance of rote procedures (McKnight et al., 1987, p. 81).

Two recent major studies called attention to this problem. Ernest Boyer's (1983) study of U.S. high schools found an over-abundance of teaching consisting of the transmittal of "fragments of information, unexamined and unanalyzed."

Boyer notes:

> The pressure is on to teach the skills that can be counted and reported. As one teacher said, "We are so hung up on reporting measured gains to the community or nationally normed tests that we ignore teaching those areas where it can't be done."

Similarly, John Goodlad (1984) found in his massive study of more than 1,000 U.S. classrooms that for the most part, "the curriculum appeared to call for and make appropriate only some ways of knowing and learning and not others." He found that students listen, read short sections in textbooks, respond briefly to questions, and take short-answer or multiple-choice quizzes. They rarely plan or initiate anything, create their own products, read or write anything substantial, or engage in analytic discussions. And there are few incentives for their teachers to pursue these approaches.

As Goodlad comments:

> Teachers are sensitive to the pressures that state and district testing programs place on them. They get the message. The other messages—that there are goals beyond those that the tests measure, that pursuing such goals calls for alternative teaching strategies, that the fundamentals of the curriculum transcend grade-level requirements—are faint to begin with, and they are drowned out by the more immediate and stronger message . . .

As a recent study of the implementation of California's new mathematics curriculum points out, when a curriculum reform aimed at problem solving and the development of higher order thinking skills encounters an already mandated rote-oriented basic skills testing program, the tests win out (Cohen et al., 1990; Darling-Hammond, 1990).

As one teacher put it:

Teaching for understanding is what we are supposed to be doing
. . . (but) the bottom line here is that all they really want to know
is how are these kids doing on the tests? . . . They want me to
teach in a way that they can't test, except that I'm held accountable to the test. It's a Catch 22. . . . (Wilson, 1990)

These studies point out how important it is for schools to
choose their "accountability tools" carefully. Clearly, if performance measures are actually to support meaningful learning,
they must assess and encourage valuable kinds of teaching in
classrooms.

WHAT ARE THE ALTERNATIVES?

Assessment in most other countries is substantially different
from the kind of multiple-choice testing common in the United
States. Not unlike the Advanced Placement tests taken by a
small minority of U.S. seniors, high school students in most Eu-
ropean countries complete extended essay examinations, often
coupled with oral examinations, in a range of subjects requiring
serious critical thought. The French Baccalaureate, for example,
asks such questions as: "What is judgment?" and, "Why should
we defend the weak?" These are a far cry from the kind of thinking required of most U.S. students, who use a number two pencil to fill in fixed-response bubbles aimed at identifying a single
right answer.

Other countries' assessments also include practical performance events requiring students to plan, implement, and/or
evaluate various tasks, such as the use of scientific procedures or
the conduct of a social research project.

Some assessments involve the guided development of cumulative portfolios of student work which shape learning opportunities and classroom evaluation over the course of a year
or more. Graduates in England submit such portfolios, along
with written examinations in three of their chosen areas of spe-
cialty. The other exhibitions and oral examinations in which
they participate are designed to provide many and varied opportunities for them to display their best work, while allowing
their teachers and outside examiners opportunities to probe the
nature and quality of their thinking.

In most of these countries, there is also a different notion of the role of educators in assessment. Faculties convene to develop and score the assessments. Teachers are involved in examining their own students and those of teachers in other schools. In many cases, much of the assessment process is internal, in the sense that it is under the control of the teacher and directly tied to ongoing instruction. In these ways, the act of assessment improves knowledge, practice, and shared standards across the educational enterprise as a whole, among the professional faculty and the students.

> The act of assessment improves knowledge, practice, and shared standards across the educational enterprise as a whole.

What separates these assessment strategies from the forms of testing more traditional in the United States? According to Wiggins (1989), authentic tests have four basic characteristics in common. First, they are designed to be truly representative of performance in the field. Students actually *do* writing—for real audiences—rather than taking spelling tests or answering questions about writing. They *conduct* science experiments rather than memorizing disconnected facts about science. The tasks are contextualized, complex intellectual challenges involving the student's own research or use of knowledge in "ill-structured" tasks requiring the development and use of meta-cognitive skills. They also allow appropriate room for student learning styles, aptitudes, and interests to serve as a source for developing competence and for the identification of (perhaps previously hidden) strengths.

Second, the criteria used in the assessment seek to evaluate "essentials" of performance against well-articulated performance standards that are openly expressed to students and others in the learning community, rather than kept secret in the tradition of content-based examinations. These criteria represent a standard because they are based on explicit and shared schoolwide aims, and they are multifaceted, representing the various aspects of a task, rather than reduced to a single grade.

Because the criteria are performance-oriented (e.g., demonstrated ability to evaluate competing viewpoints and evidence in developing a persuasive essay concerning a topic of social importance), they guide teaching, learning, and evaluation in a way that illuminates the goals and processes of learning, placing teachers in the role of coach and students in the role of performers as well as self-evaluators.

As suggested above, the third characteristic is that self-assessment plays an important role in authentic tasks. A major goal of authentic assessment is to help students develop the capacity to evaluate their own work against public standards; to revise, modify, and redirect their energies, taking initiative to assess their own progress.

> A major goal of authentic assessment is to help students develop the capacity to evaluate their own work against public standards.

This is a major aspect of self-directed work and self-motivated improvement required of all human beings in real-world situations. Because performance standards take the concept of progress seriously—making the processes of refinement and improvement of products a central aspect of the task and its evaluation—they also allow students of all initial levels of developed competence the opportunity to see, acknowledge, and receive credit for their own growth.

Finally, the students are generally expected to present their work and defend themselves publicly and orally to ensure that their apparent mastery is genuine. This characteristic of authentic assessment serves other goals as well—signaling to students that their work is important enough to be a source of public learning and celebration; providing opportunities for others in the learning community—students, faculty, and parents—to continually examine, refine, learn from, and appreciate shared goals and achievements; and creating living representations of the purposes and standards of the learning community so that they remain vital and energizing.

A number of schools, including members of the Coalition of Essential Schools founded by Theodore Sizer (1984; 1992), are engaged in creating authentic assessments of student learning. A growing number of states—including Vermont, California, Connecticut, and New York—are developing new approaches to assessment that will transform statewide testing. Teachers in Vermont are developing student portfolios in writing and mathematics as the basis of their state's assessment system.

Connecticut and New York have begun to develop performance-based assessments that require students to perform a science experiment or solve a real-world problem using mathematical and scientific concepts rather than complete a multiple-choice test. California, Maryland, and several other states have developed writing assessments based on student essays. Some of these engage students in complex writing tasks requiring several days of work, including revisions, as part of the examination process. Districts such as Shoreham-Wading River, N.Y.; Pittsburgh, Pa.; New York City and Rochester, N.Y.; and Albuquerque, N. Mex., are also creating authentic assessment to take the place of standardized testing.

Initiatives such as these are an attempt to make schools genuinely accountable for helping students to acquire the kinds of higher order skills and abilities they will need to use in the world outside school. As the Coalition of Essential Schools (1990) explains:

> Of course we want students who are curious, who know how to approach new problems, who use reading and writing across the disciplines as a natural part of that process, who are thoughtful, able, and active citizens. And to get them we (should) make those goals known from the start, test for them regularly, and correct a student's course when necessary.

In addition to helping teachers and students to evaluate what the students can really do, these approaches serve as expressive tools for students and are highly motivating. Sizer points out that they are as much inspiration as measurement: "Giving kids a really good target is the best way to teach them . . . And if the goal is cast in an interesting way, you greatly increase the chances of their achieving it" (Coalition of Essential Schools, 1990).

As a testament to Sizer's claim, every one of the 1991 graduates of Central Park East Secondary School went on to postsecondary education, and 92 percent of them were accepted to four-year colleges, a rate more than twice as high as surrounding area high schools.

One student explained their success in terms of the authenticity of goals set and performances achieved: "This environment gives us standards. It makes us look at ourselves in the mirror and feel proud of our accomplishments."

REFERENCES

Archbald, Doug A., and Newman, Fred M. *Beyond Standardized Testing: Assessing Authentic Academic Achievement in the Secondary School.* Reston, Va.: National Association of Secondary School Principals, 1988.

Boyer, Ernest. *High School.* New York: Harper and Row, 1983.

Coalition of Essential Schools. "Performances and Exhibitions: The Demonstration of Mastery." *Horace,* March 1990.

Cohen, David, et al. "Case Studies of Curriculum Implementation." *Educational Evaluation and Policy Analysis,* Fall 1990.

Darling-Hammond, Linda. "Instructional Policy into Practice: The Power of the Bottom Over the Top." *Educational Evaluation and Policy Analysis,* Fall 1990.

Darling-Hammond, Linda, and Wise, Arthur E. "Beyond Standardization: State Standards and School Improvement." *The Elementary School Journal* 3(1985): 315–36.

Drucker, Peter F. *The Frontiers of Management.* New York: Harper and Row, 1986.

Goodlad, John. *A Place Called School: Prospects for the Future.* New York: McGraw-Hill, 1984.

Hudson Institute. *Workforce 2000: Work and Workers for the 21st Century.* Indianapolis, Ind.: Hudson Institute, 1987.

Haney, Walt, and Madaus, George. "Effects of Standardized Testing and the Future of the National Assessment of Educational Progress." Working paper for the NAEP study group. Chestnut Hill, Mass.: Center for the Study of Testing, Evaluation and Educational Policy, 1986.

Koretz, Daniel. "Arriving in Lake Wobegon: Are Standardized Tests Exaggerating Achievement and Distorting Instruction?" *American Educator,* 2(1988): 8–15, 46–52.

LaPointe, Archie E., et al. *A World of Differences: An International Assessment of Mathematics and Science.* Princeton, N.J.: ETS, 1989.

McKnight, C. C., Crosswhite, F. J., Dossey, J. A., Kifer, E., Swafford, S. O., Travers, K. J., and Cooney, T. J. *The Underachieving Curriculum: Assessing U.S. School Mathematics from an International Perspective.* Champaign, Ill.: Stipes Publishing, 1987.

National Assessment for Educational Progress. *Reading, Thinking, and Writing: Results from the 1979–80 National Assessment of Reading and Literature.* Denver, Colo.: NAEP, 1981.

National Research Council. *Ability Testing: Uses, Consequences, and Controversies.* Edited by Alexander K. Wigdor and Wendell R. Garner. Washington, D.C.: National Academy Press, 1982.

Resnick, Lauren B. *Education and Learning to Think.* Washington, D.C.: National Academy Press, 1987.

Sizer, Theodore. *Horace's Compromise: The Dilemma of the American High School.* Boston, Mass.: Houghton Mifflin, 1984.

———. *Horace's School.* Boston, Mass.: Houghton Mifflin, 1992.

Sternberg, Robert J. *Beyond IQ.* New York: Cambridge University Press, 1985.

Wiggins, Grant. "Teaching to the (Authentic) Test." *Educational Leadership,* April 1989.

Wilson, Suzanne. "A Conflict of Interests: Constraints That Affect Teaching and Change." *Educational Evaluation and Policy Analysis,* Fall 1990.

Portfolio Assessment and the New Paradigm: New Instruments and New Places

by Brenda S. Engel

T he health and survival of progressive educational practice may well depend on teachers knowing and explaining—to themselves and to others—the rationale behind the methods they use to teach and the ways they select to assess student progress. Contemporary meaning-based pedagogies that view the learner as an active seeker and constructor (rather than a passive receiver) of knowledge require rethinking the instruction-curriculum-assessment triad. Constructivism and whole language, for instance—along with what one might call whole science, whole art, whole social studies, or, collectively, whole education—will remain vulnerable to fads unless theory and practice are closely and intentionally interactive on the classroom level, with theory guiding practice and practice modifying theory continually.

> Contemporary meaning-based pedagogies . . . require rethinking the instruction-curriculum-assessment triad.

We all recognize the signs of danger: whole language explained as "using big books to teach reading," invented spelling reduced to "letting children make spelling mistakes," or new math curricula described as "the use of manipulatives in the early grades." When some of the superficial, highly visible char-

From *The Educational Forum*, vol. 59, no. 1, Fall 1994, pp. 22–27. © 1994 by Kappa Delta Pi. Reprinted with permission.

acteristics of new theory and practice become definitions, we are in danger of losing the whole progressive enterprise and of creating the conditions for a pendulum swing back to basics.

NEW PARADIGM IN EDUCATION

Education is presently undergoing a shift in paradigm. Kuhn (1970, 111), who first explored the concept of paradigm shifts, wrote:

> Examining the record of past research from the vantage of con-
> temporary historiography, the historian of science may be
> tempted to exclaim that when paradigms change, the world itself
> changes with them. Led by a new paradigm, scientists adopt new
> instruments and look in new places.

Although Kuhn confined his discussion of paradigm change to the field of science, others have applied the term more broadly. Emig (1982, 64), in a paper on student writing, described the fundamental character of a paradigm as a "governing gaze." Poplin (1988, 389), in an article on special education, quoted Heshusius's useful distinction between paradigm and theory:

> The concept of paradigm then is far more encompassing than
> that of theory. . . . While theory directly delineates the phenom-
> ena of interest, a paradigm does not, but rather presents a world
> view, a "way of seeing" which is also a way of not seeing. It repre-
> sent the beliefs by which we ultimately think and act.

The new paradigm in education is a more focused "governing gaze," "world view," or "way of seeing." This emphasis on meaning as the energizing force behind learning necessitates new methods of assessment (using "new instruments" and looking in "new places"). This article discusses that shift, sug-gests its potential significance for classroom teachers, and builds a case for portfolio assessment as a logical concomitant of the new paradigm.

The influence of the new paradigm can be seen in the whole language and process writing movements, in the National Council of Teachers of Mathematics Standards, in hands-on science, and in the multiple perspectives in the new social stud-ies. Personal meaning is stressed in these areas of the curriculum—meaning not transmitted from teacher to learner but, rather, constructed by each learner, with the teacher serving as mentor and guide. An individual constructs meaning, a group or culture constructs meaning—but one person or group cannot create meaning for another.

The arts can virtually be *defined* as the creation of meaning. In all forms, the arts demands originality and the infusion of self and personal meaning. Only when children are given patterns or models to copy does art lose its educational, meaning-making value. This attention to meaning is not new—some of these ideas have existed for a couple of centuries. But they now have a pervasive presence that can be seen as a genuine paradigm shift.

> It takes time and effort for most people to accept new ideas and to support teachers in unfamiliar practices.

Adjusting to a shift in paradigms—to changes in beliefs and practices—can be difficult, even painful, because of the strength of habit and history, and the forces of inertia. Some administrators, community members, representatives of the media, teachers, and parents are eager to explore new ways of thinking about teaching and learning. Others are skeptical or actively resistant.

Parents, who often have the most immediate, vested interest in education, can be particularly wary of change. They tend to call upon their own experiences with school, and rely on the familiar and traditional—even in cases where their own experiences had been largely negative. Their uneasiness is manifested in comments such as, "Why do you allow him to make all those mistakes in spelling? I'm embarrassed to show his papers to his grandparents"; or "She's not really reading it; she knows that book already." It takes effort and explanation to communicate to parents the thinking behind "invented spelling" or "emergent reading." It takes time and effort, in fact, for most people to accept new ideas and to support teachers in unfamiliar practices.

NEW RESPONSIBILITIES FOR TEACHERS

There are two primary reasons that teachers must develop a basic grasp of theory: first, for purposes of communication—so that they can clearly and confidently explain the rationale for new practices to other teachers, administrators, parents, and concerned members of the public; and second, as a self-correcting guide to practice—so teachers understand why they are doing what they are doing and do not mistake the signs for the substance: Big books do not whole language make.

At a time when teacher power seems to be increasing, it is important that teachers seize the opportunity to be knowledgeable, independent, and creative. They should be free to invent and improvise methods and materials according to their knowledge of how children learn. This knowledge must be interpreted for the particular conditions that exist in each classroom—the setting where theory and practice interact.

The three basic elements of classroom practice—pedagogy, curriculum, and assessment—are closely interrelated and are all affected by the changes in beliefs that constitute the new paradigm. Beliefs bring responsibilities. If one believes that knowledge is essentially constructed rather than received by the learner, there are unavoidable implications concerning what is taught, how it is taught, and how learning is assessed: what is taught needs to build on or be connected to what the student already knows. The primary task of assessment, then, is to inform instruction: To explore and define what the student knows and can do in order to plan further learning.

NEW TYPES OF ASSESSMENT

The primary purpose of judgmental assessment, which relies on standardized testing, is to sort and evaluate students. This kind of testing contributes little information useful for instruction. Now, with ideals of universal access and the assumption that all children can be successful school learners, the picture is changing. Authentic assessment, associated with meaning-based pedagogies, implies assessment practices that contribute directly to classroom instruction and to education.

The meaning of "authentic," which has become an automatically honorific term in educational assessment, is not always clear. According to *Webster's Ninth New Collegiate Dictionary* (1991), authentic means "worthy of acceptance or belief, trustworthy." It should be added that authentic implies something that is as it seems. An authentic gold piece, for instance, is one you can trust because it not only appears to be gold, but actually is gold. Authentic behavior implies that a person is acting as he or she feels.

Authenticity can be seen as consistency in time—between what is happening now and what is intended for the future. An action is authentic when aligned with its long-term purposes—when one can look toward the future and see the connection between the means and the end. In assessment, authenticity implies that the results can be trusted partly because the methods support long-term purposes. Authenticity can be contrasted with expediency. The former is justified by a long-term view; the latter by a short-term perceived need.

> In assessment, authenticity implies that the results can be trusted partly because the methods support long-term purposes.

Classroom assessment is moving from expediency (i.e., standardized testing) toward authenticity. It is assuming broader responsibilities and a somewhat different mission: to assist teachers, schools, and school systems in accepting children wherever and whoever they are, and to provide them with equal access to education and with the means to live up to their potential.

If these responsibilities are taken seriously, they have strong implications for how we assess students' progress. The words "whoever they are" must be emphasized—it is not the school's task to shape, form, or develop character. Children come to school with their characters fairly well formed and, in any event, their characters belong to them, and are their private property. The school's task, rather, is to provide children with access to education—to help them build bridges between the world of home and home culture and the world of school and school culture.

Children should be able to cross those bridges with their characters and sense of self intact. If they have to leave a large piece of themselves at home, they come to school weakened and are likely to become alienated, ineffectual learners. Alienation is associated, in the extensive literature on the subject, with dropouts, school failure, and misbehavior. "Whoever they are" includes physical appearance, ways of learning, feelings, past experiences, cast of mind, and interests. This does not refer to behavior as such—it goes without saying that disruptive behavior must be controlled and children have to learn to live within the *necessary* (i.e., not arbitrary) expectations of the classroom community. Nevertheless, children need to be respected for who they are, rather than for what we want them to be.

> Children need to be respected for who they are, rather than for what we want them to be.

Authentic assessment is meant to help teachers and children work together in the most productive ways possible. It is meant to facilitate effective communication with parents. One scheme, described by Engel, Hall, and Stuart (in press) proposed two parallel collections of data, one created by the teacher and one by the student. The teacher's collection includes curriculum notes, observations, reflections on individual students or on the classroom as a whole, notes on parent conferences, test results, and whatever else that teacher normally keeps. The student's collection—the portfolio—includes work samples from all areas of the curriculum. Both collections inform the student profile, the report that is sent to parents.

Returning to questions of authenticity and the need for bridges between home and school, what are we examining when we assess children's learning? Because of their obviousness rather than their importance, we might first look at skills—handwriting, word spacing, directionality in reading, number facts, and so on. Second, we might also be interested in the student's control over information—the kinds of dinosaurs that existed in North America, the names of common colors, the number of states in New England, etc. Third, we are interested in higher-level skills and understanding—of the metamorphosis of butterflies; the electrical connections between batteries, wires, and bulbs; the laws of probability in math; or why violence is not a rational solution to disagreements. Finally, and perhaps most importantly, we are interested in personal characteristics and habits of mind: curiosity, inventiveness, willingness to take risks, self-confidence, sociability, and so on.

In real life all of these aspects of learning are woven seamlessly together. Why is it, then, that the first two—skills and information—are the usual subjects of testing? The answer:

Skills and information are easier to extract because they can be tested out of context. Who is the president of the United States? Bill Clinton. What does two plus two equal? Four. What color results from mixing blue and yellow? Green. This is the kind of subject matter that lends itself to testing (although the same kind of information can be ascertained through portfolios). Higher-level skills are more difficult to test through multiple-choice formats because they depend on creative thinking and divergent solutions. Habits of mind cannot be tested at all out of context, yet are central to the whole learning process. There is no test for curiosity, for example, because curiosity must be seen in context—curiosity about *something*. As a characteristic, however, curiosity is of enormous importance to learning.

> **Habits of mind cannot be tested at all out of context, yet are central to the whole learning process.**

Personal characteristics and habits of mind are not always developmental or school-acquired. They come with the child. They either cross the bridge with him or her from home or, if not recognized, appreciated, or allowed expression in school, they may soon be left outside the school door. Some children are tougher and more insistent on bringing who they are into the classroom. Others are easily discouraged and often lose character when they enter the school setting. (There are, of course, children from all classes and backgrounds whose characters have already been assaulted at home.)

PORTFOLIOS REVEAL STUDENTS

Learning characteristics and habits of mind are evident in student portfolios. Statements of self come in many forms, as children reveal themselves through their work: "This is me"; "I am here"; "This is my hand you see the traces of, my perspective, my humor, my interest." Some examples:

> Bethann painted a picture, from life, of a bowl of daffodils. In her picture the daffodils were bright blue with purple leaves. When asked about the colors, Bethann said matter-of-factly that she just liked them that way.
> (An assertion of taste.)

Anton wrote a detailed, play-by-play story about a game between the Boston Celtics and the New York Knicks—the handwriting becoming more and more scrawled. Finally, on page three, he broke off the account and addressed the reader directly: "It's too long so I will tell you who won. Boston won."
(An assumption of the reader's interest in his, Anton's, story, and that the reader would want to hear the ending.)

Pencil drawings in Francisco's portfolio show his interest in things electric or electronic—video games, radios, TV sets, refrigerators—all of which he draws skillfully and in detail. He also practices his drawing skill, covering pages with boxes, drawn in perspective, and schematic stars.
(A child is bringing to school his preoccupation with drawing and his fascination with a particular subject matter.)

Letter: Dear Editor, In one of your stories, "How Mom Saved the Planet," it says that everyone has a mom. But that is not true. You can have one dad, no mom, or two dads, no mom, or just a grandmother etc. love, Eric.
(This was not actually written in school but uses new ability learned in school to communicate understanding of the social world.)

Arthur's story: When paper got burnt I always used to think it was burnt butterflies. Sometimes when I smell fire, I think of Boston and foggy things.
(Taking risks by writing private thoughts and feelings.)

Book by Rachel, grade 1: I can pante, yes I can. I can clim a tree, yes I can. I can feed my dolls, yes I can. I can brayd my hair, yes I can. I can bild a bloc tawor, yes I can. I can help my mommy, yes I can. I can play with my frends, yes I can. I can go sleding, yes I can. I can go to bed all by myself.
(Sense of self.)

These are examples of children being themselves in school. Many children, unfortunately, are inexpressive in school, saving energy and personal investment for out-of-school activities—sports, friends, family, and TV. Their alienation from school is evident in their portfolios, which are usually not particularly interesting or fun to read. There seems to be no one there.

Characteristics and habits of mind, although not always acquired in school, can, nonetheless, be sustained there. Curiosity, confidence, and imagination must be recognized, valued, and given opportunity for expression. These are the sources of energy, not only for school learning, but for lifelong learning. They are the characteristics that most children bring with them when they enter kindergarten and are most likely to be supported in such settings—where rooms are full of materials and opportunities for expression of self.

Deborah Meier (1993), educator and founder of Central Park East Elementary and Central Park East Secondary Schools in New York City, said that kindergarten should provide the model for education throughout the grades. Perhaps she was referring to the fact that kindergarten children are encouraged to explore, create, and learn, all at once, and that education should be an opportunity, not an imposition as it often becomes when children move into the early grades. Motivation to learn should come from the child's own curiosity and drive to explore, to understand, to connect with and exert a degree of control over, the culture of the school—the child's stand-in for the culture of the larger world.

Portfolios can capture and reveal significant aspects of personal meaning. When cumulative portfolios are kept from kindergarten on, they help children retain both confidence in who they are and a sense of identity—requisites for becoming effective learners in school. When reviewing portfolios with children, teachers find that they are indeed using "new instruments and looking in new places." The new instruments are the portfolios themselves. The new places are the products of the active, creative, energetic, imaginative, constructive, and meaning-making minds of children.

REFERENCES

Emig, J. 1982. Inquiry paradigms and writing. *College Composition and Communication* 33(1): 64–75.

Engel, B. S., L. Hall, and L. Stuart, eds. In press. *The Cambridge handbook on documentation and assessment: Child portfolios and teacher records in the primary grades.* North Dakota Study Group monograph. Grand Forks, N.D.: University of North Dakota Press.

Heshusius, L. 1987. Traditional concepts of science and special education: Contours of possibilities for alternatives. A paradigmatic overview. Unpublished manuscript. Toronto, Canada: York University.

Kuhn, T. S. 1970. *The structure of scientific revolutions.* Chicago: University of Chicago Press.

Meier, D. 1993. Personal communication. November.

Poplin, M. 1988. The reductionist fallacy in learning disabilities: Replicating the past by reducing the present. *Journal of Learning Disabilities* 21(7): 389–400.

Assessing Portfolios Using the Constructivist Paradigm

by F. Leon Paulson and Pearl R. Paulson

I n 1990, we participated in a conference on portfolio assessment sponsored by the Northwest Evaluation Association. The topic of the conference was aggregating portfolio data. By way of preparation, we wrote a paper called *How Do Portfolios Measure Up? A Cognitive Model for Assessing Portfolios* [CMAP] (Paulson and Paulson, 1990). In our paper, we offered an assessment model loosely based on Robert Stake's (1967) evaluation model, one that could report descriptive or numerical material in ways that allowed educational activities to be assessed in context (see also Paulson and Paulson, 1991; Paulson, Paulson, and Frazier, in press).

> **Portfolios are by nature complex and holistic pictures of a child's learning. . . .**

There were two reasons for creating this model. One was that we wanted an assessment model that would be comprehensive. Portfolios are by nature complex and holistic pictures of a child's learning and we wanted to provide an analysis model that preserved as much complexity as possible. Second, we were concerned about the aggregation of portfolio data. Efforts to aggregate data usually involve standardizing the events being aggregated. Our concern was that attempts to aggregate might change the very thing being aggregated. Thus, the second concern of our model was to be able to document the impact of the aggregation itself.

Paper presented at the annual meeting of the American Educational Research Association (New Orleans, LA, April 4–8, 1994). © 1994 by F. Leon Paulson and Pearl R. Pauslon. Reprinted with permission.

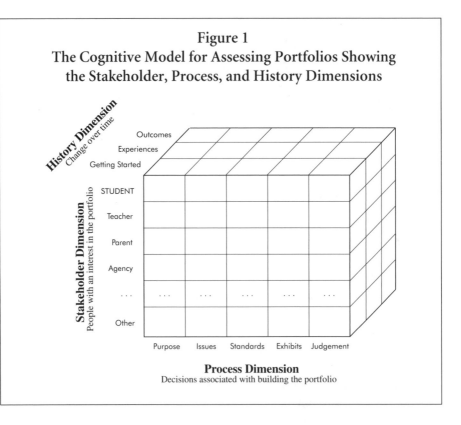

Figure 1
The Cognitive Model for Assessing Portfolios Showing the Stakeholder, Process, and History Dimensions

We intended CMAP as a means of describing portfolios and portfolio projects in context rather than as a cookbook for conducting portfolio assessments. Thus, CMAP was designed to be a lens to view, think about, and make decisions about portfolio projects.

CMAP views a portfolio simultaneously from three perspective or dimensions—(1) people influencing or being influenced by the portfolio (stakeholders), (2) activities involved in constructing the portfolio (process), and (3) the record of change it presents over time (history). These relations are represented visually in Figure 1.

Two educators representing very different perspectives contacted us to say they were using CMAP in designing portfolio projects. Margaret Jorgensen, a researcher associated with the Atlanta office of the Educational Testing Service, told us that she was using a somewhat modified version of CMAP to design an authentic assessment project in math and science that she was proposing for the National Science Foundation. She invited us to be consultants to the project. Anita Rutlin, an associate superintendent of the Wyoming, Michigan, School District, told us that the Wyoming district was making substantial changes in the way they conducted assessment and that she was using CMAP for guidance.

Both projects were concerned that assessment be more authentic.

We tracked the development of these two projects with interest and, in the process, have become aware that they offer an interesting and instructive contrast. Both projects involve a multidimensional approach implied in the model. Yet, the differences in the way the model is interpreted are sharp. The Atlanta model (Jorgensen, 1993, 1994) is probably more familiar to those in educational research and development. It comes out of a long tradition of research and development: goals are established; work schedules set; and activities are carefully managed, monitored, and reported. In contrast, the Wyoming model (Rutlin, personal communication) is probably more familiar to practitioners concerned with ongoing educational programs. Like the Atlanta model, the Wyoming model is driven by a clear philosophic direction, but unlike the Atlanta model, management is decentralized and there is an expectation that the territory is unmapped and the route indirect. Let us take a look at some of the contrasts between the two projects.

A COMPARISON OF CONTRASTING PORTFOLIO PROJECTS
Overall Design
Both projects were concerned that assessment be more authentic even when large numbers of students were involved. Both were guided by a specific philosophy. While Atlanta was concerned with supporting teacher-assessment of many students across districts, Wyoming, Michigan, was concerned with supporting self-assessment by many students within its district. Atlanta was guided by a philosophy that placed priority on providing good assessment; Wyoming, Michigan, was guided by a philosophy that placed priority on supporting classroom learning.

For the Atlanta project, ETS developed an assessment plan, obtained necessary letters of support from local school districts, and submitted a proposal describing the project and how it would be implemented. The Atlanta model was designed to encourage input from stakeholders. The project called for assembling teams of teachers from the six participating districts. Its kickoff was a workshop during which teams selected curriculum goals that were common to all districts. The teams then developed definitions that became the design specifications for performance tasks, also developed by teachers. The majority of the assessment tasks would allow teachers to use content from their local district curriculum or even materials specially tailored to student needs or interests. Each task would yield concrete material suitable for inclusion in portfolios. Students would develop portfolios by completing a prescribed set of performance assessments. As the project proceeded, project staff sought input from stakeholders in the field of science and education, and took steps to make parents more fully aware of the project.

The Wyoming, Michigan, project began with a set of General Learner Outcomes adopted by the district's school board. These were general philosophical statements of what constitutes an educated student, which in turn identified curriculum areas that students would be expected to master during their years in school. While the general outcomes were set by the school board, there was a clear philosophy that the process of reaching those goals would be as decentralized as possible. In addition to expecting its students to demonstrate that they have achieved each outcome, Wyoming expected them to interpret the outcomes in ways that are personally meaningful. The teachers provide a curriculum that offers information and experiences that allow students to interpret the outcomes in a knowledgeable and socially responsible manner, and help them gather evidence for their portfolios. Michigan, like most states, publishes a large curriculum document describing goals and objectives for students at each grade level and holds districts legally accountable for their attainment. In the Wyoming district, copies of this document are placed in each classroom as a resource document for *both* teachers and students. Teachers refer to this document as they prepare lesson plans and students refer to [it] as they make decisions about the competencies they document through

Table 1		
A Comparison of the Two Projects		
	Atlanta, Georgia	**Wyoming, Michigan**
General Approach	To achieve consensus on general and specific outcomes to guide instruction and assessment.	To provide a philosophical context to guide instruction and assessment.
General Goals	Example Goal: *To develop students who are* - *effective collaborators* - *creative and strategic* - *reflective thinkers and self-evaluators* - *self-motivated learners* - *effective communicators* - *responsible global citizens*	General Learner Outcomes: *Effective communicator* - *complex thinker* - *creative thinker* - *problem solver* *Self-directed learner* *Contributor to well being* *Cooperative worker* *Effective citizen*
Specific Goals and Standards	Project staff and teachers further define each goal, seeking an operational level, e.g., "collaborators": - *recognizes self-worth and that of others* - *believes that the collaborative result will be better than any single effort* - *demonstrates respect for self and others by accepting responsibility for collaborative participation* - *recognizes the right of all members to participate and have a vote*	Goals supplied to teachers and students who further define and operationalize. (District provides training and support.)
Evidence of Attaining Goal in Relation to Standard	Group creates rubric to score examples of student work. Examples come from tasks designed by teams of teachers at the district level. The portfolio is a collection of the tasks. Students may or may not select the contents of their portfolios.	The General Learner Outcomes are used in the classroom as teachers and students develop rubrics and set standards. Students in collaboration with teachers select evidence of the achievement of the goals. Students select the items that go into the portfolios.
Judgment	Trained teams of teachers score products on an individual basis. Psychometric standards apply to ensuring the validity of the process.	A complex judgment is made that includes the student as a self-assessor, peers, teacher, parents, and eventually people from the community who judge the students' portfolios.

their portfolios. Table 1 (see p. 31) summarizes the similarities and contrasts between the two programs.

Stakeholders

An interesting question concerns what one means by stakeholder. One way of using the term would be as a way to refer to those who are interested and who the project must address as an *audience*. Another way of looking at stakeholders is to consider them as individuals who play an active role as *participants* in shaping the project. Let us look more closely at the contrasts between the Atlanta and the Wyoming approaches. Both projects focused on CMAP's stakeholder dimension as a place from which to start. The Atlanta project saw stakeholders (teachers, students, parents) as relatively discrete groups that districts could involve independently at many points in the process. For example, they decided to involve parents during the second year.

> Parents were often included in the earliest discussions and some parts of the program were suggested by parents.

Wyoming, in contrast, tended to involve all stakeholders from the beginning. Parents were often included in the earliest discussions and some parts of the program were suggested by parents. They began training individual teachers on portfolio processes and ideas but left the implementation of those ideas to the classroom. Gradually, through a process that was more evolutionary than anything else, certain practices emerged as more viable than others and were adopted in more and more classrooms.

Setting Specific Instructional Goals

In the Atlanta project, each performance assessment produced information reflecting the curricular goal decided on by the centralized agency, a consensual decision by representatives of six school districts. The teams of teachers from participating districts assumed the challenge of defining the outcome goals in more and more specific terms and specifying processes and activities that would be used in all districts. These test-like situations sometimes used prescribed math and science content and sometimes allowed teachers to insert content from their own curriculum.[1] For example, an assessment task might call for scientific observation, but just what the student was observing might vary from classroom to classroom. In all cases, the activities prescribed what materials students would generate for their portfolios. The process was reminiscent of developing test items, only the items were performance assessments that could take place in the classroom.

In contrast, Wyoming provided its teachers with the most general statements of outcomes and invited them to translate them into classroom practice. No specific curriculum and no specific test-like situations were implied or described. Rather, teachers were encouraged to share the general outcomes with their students, and students working with teachers were encouraged to come up with definitions that were meaningful to the individuals involved. For example, one of the general learner outcomes was "cooperation." The district said only that students were required to learn to become cooperative citizens. It was the responsibility of the teacher and the students to interpret the outcome and decide what evidence might be presented in order to show that this outcome was attained. Part of the learning for the student was to interpret the goal and to make it operational.

> **Everything in the [Atlanta] project was either planned in advance or modified from an existing plan.**

Project Management

Project management also provides an interesting contrast. The Atlanta project was carefully managed and executed. Everything in the project was either planned in advance or modified from an existing plan. The Wyoming project, in contrast, seems to have "just grown" around a central philosophy of student ownership. The Wyoming approach became self-perpetuating in an intriguing way. The State of Michigan offered a series of small grants to support innovative educational programs. Anita Rutlin posted the notice of this grant on the district high school's bulletin board with a note saying that maybe these funds could be used to develop a handbook to help students put together portfolios. She received a response not from teachers but from students. The students, who thought having such a handbook would be valuable, wrote the proposal with Rutlin's encouragement and help. The proposal eventually became the first that the State of Michigan had awarded to a student initiated project. The students have completed the high school handbook and it is in use throughout the district. Parents requested a similar handbook for their elementary age children. A committee of parents, elementary teachers, and high school students prepared an elementary version based on the one developed by the high school students (Wyoming, 1993).

Performance Standards

A major contrast between the two projects involves the setting of standards. In the Atlanta project, standards were set by the teams of teachers who developed consensual rubrics that permitted student work to be judged in a reliable fashion. One of the chief concerns of the project was to develop assessment tasks that could be used over a variety of instructional activities and classrooms. The same teachers who developed activities also developed the rubrics. To refine the rubrics, they repeatedly collected and judged student responses. The rubrics and the training procedures were refined until all teachers and project consultants felt that they had achieved reliable measurement (defined as rater agreement). The rubrics were then field tested with different teachers and in other districts. Often the tasks were used across different instructional settings. Again, the characteristics were refined until a satisfactory level of rater agreement was observed. At that point the rubrics were offered for general use throughout the six participating districts and will be published for adoption anywhere.

> A major contrast between the two projects involves the setting of standards.

Wyoming also encouraged the use of rubrics, but left design of the rubrics to the people in the classroom. For example, a state outcome has to do with cooperation (see Table 1). One teacher had her class brainstorm the characteristics of what they thought a cooperative person was. Another teacher taught a short story unit by first distributing examples of short stories (found in literature as well as collected from the previous year's students) and had the students analyze the stories and generate statements characterizing good short stories. Each student then wrote an individual rubric to be used to judge their own writing during the remainder of the short story unit. In both cases, the rubrics were used for self-assessment, peer-assessment, and teacher-assessment in a way reminiscent of the *quality-control circle* found in Deming's writings (Deming, 1986), in which students were participants both in setting and applying standards. Students revised their rubrics throughout the year as their understanding grew, and as their performance improved so did their standards. Thus, standards here are (1) individual to each student, (2) appropriate to the level of performance of each student, and (3) moving upward. The process is consistent with Deming's philosophy of quality control, in which quality is controlled locally, not by centralized authority (see Deming, 1986; Gitlow and Gitlow, 1987; Paulson, 1993).

TOWARD A CONSTRUCTIVIST MODEL FOR ASSESSING PORTFOLIOS

What do we learn from examining these two projects? First, the challenge of describing them is quite different. The Atlanta project's clear focus is on student outcomes of instruction and the entire project is systematically designed to produce student outcomes that lend themselves to summarization across individuals and across groups. Standard evaluation techniques found in most textbooks are well suited to analyzing this project. The Wyoming project's focus was far more diverse. There were outcomes, but they were very generally defined— certainly not in terms that lend themselves to measurement as we usually think of it. Much of the approach was designed by students and teachers as they went along, guided less by a specific assessment design than a clear statement of philosophy regarding instruction and learning.

Contrasting Paradigms: Positivism and Constructivism

The contrast here is between two models of assessment: the one (represented by Atlanta) we call positivist, the other (represented by Wyoming) we call constructivist (see Lincoln and Guba, 1985, p. 14ff, for a discussion contrasting these two approaches). Let us briefly define these two paradigms.

Positivist

The purpose of the portfolio is to assess learning outcomes and those outcomes are, generally, defined externally. Positivism assumes that meaning is constant across users, contexts, and purposes (making it reasonable, for example, to think about national and even "world-class" standards). The portfolio is a receptacle for examples of student work used to infer what and how much learning has occurred.

> **Postivism assumes that meaning is constant across users, contexts, and purposes.**

Constructivist

The portfolio is a learning environment in which the learner constructs meaning. It assumes that meaning varies across individuals, over time, and with purpose. The portfolio presents process, a record of the processes associated with the learning itself; a summation of individual portfolios would be too complex for normative description.

The two paradigms produce portfolio activities that are entirely different. Hansen (1993), in his anthropological analysis of testing, defines *test* as "a representational technique applied by an agency to an individual with the intention of gathering information" (p. 19). The positivist view of portfolios is consistent with this definition of assessment, the constructivist view is not. Hence, tensions develop around aggregation and other high stakes uses of portfolios.

　• The positivist approach puts a premium on the selection of items that reflect outside standards and interests. Thus it is appropriate to include tests or test-like representational situations designed by others. Because outside interests and standards are applied, psychometric standards of reliability (especially inter-rater agreement) are emphasized in the judgments made about the products.

　• The constructivist approach puts a premium on the selection of items that reflect learning from the student's perspective. Thus it is not appropriate to require tests or test-like representational situations. Because idiosyncratic standards play an important role, less emphasis is placed on consistency of judgments made about the products and more emphasis is placed on the perspectives represented by the judges.

Pamela Moss recently addressed the issues of how these two paradigms differ within the context of educational assessment.

> There are certain intellectual activities that standardized assessments can neither document nor promote; these include encouraging students to find their own purposes for reading and writing, encouraging teachers to make informed instructional decisions consistent with the needs of individual students, and encouraging teachers to collaborate in developing criteria and standards to evaluate their work. (1994, p. 6)

> ... most hermeneutic philosophers[2] share a holistic and integrative approach to interpretation of human phenomena that seeks to understand the whole in light of its parts, repeatedly testing interpretation against the available evidence until each of the parts can be accounted for in a coherent interpretation of the whole. (1994, p. 7)

The Challenge Posed by the New Assessments

Portfolios, prominent in the movement to find alternative means for assessing students (see, e.g., Wolf, Bixby, Glenn, and Gardner, 1992), do not fit easily into traditional concepts of how to go about assessing learning. First, portfolios change the classroom environment (e.g., see Koretz, Stecher, and Diebert, 1992; Viechnicki, Rohrer, Ambrose, and Barbour, 1992); second, they stimulate and support integrative and reflective processes during the assessment (see Moss, 1994; Paulson and Paulson, in press), thereby changing the learning being assessed. Although portfolios have the potential of providing more authentic information on student performance than other, more contrived procedures associated with testing, assessment specialists find it difficult to apply rigorous standards associated with the psychometric paradigm (see Calfee and Perfumo, 1993; Koretz, Stecher, and Deibert, 1992).

Psychometric standards such as reliability require consistency to be defined quantitatively. This consistency increases generalizability across persons and situations, thereby supporting aggregation and other high stakes uses of assessment information. However, the less standardized forms of assessment give students considerable latitude in the interpretation [of], response to, and (especially in the case of many portfolios) [actual creation of] the tasks. By doing so, they produce formidable challenges to reliability (see Koretz et al., 1993; Shavelson, Gao, and Baxter, 1993; Suen and Davey, 1990).

Moss (1994) summarizes the general findings concerning reliability and the less standardized forms of assessment:
- Reliability defined as rater agreement on a single sample produces "acceptable" levels when rater agreement is calculated and the raters are acceptably trained.
- Reliability defined as rater agreement across tasks is much more difficult to estimate.[3]

Typically, the positivist, psychometric approach aspires to reliability by scoring each piece of the portfolio much as one would a single sample. Each example of student work is scored by readers with no outside knowledge about the learner or of other readers' judgments. It also assumes that each item stands alone and is meaningful in and of itself. Inferences are based on composite scores. The interpretability of these scores rests on previous research. The scores are provided to users with guidelines for interpretation.

Often, concern for traditional measurement standards leads to pressures to make portfolios more like tests.

Users typically consider the scores in light of additional information about the individual, "although mainstream validity theory provides little guidance about how to combine such information to reach a well-warranted conclusion" (Moss, 1994, p. 7). Often, concern for traditional measurement standards leads to pressures to make portfolios more like tests and less like comprehensive learning environments (see, e.g., Koretz et al., 1993). Constructivist (hermeneutic) analysis, however, seems better suited to large-scale portfolio assessment even though rater agreement across tasks is more difficult to estimate.

The hermeneutic approach uses holistic interpretations of collected performances that seek to understand the whole in light of its parts. Items have meaning only in context and the context itself changes as an integral part of the process of making judgments. The interpretative approach benefits readers familiar with the context, which is why the hermeneutic approach often includes detailed descriptions of the project. This grounds interpretation in context and encourages conversation (occasionally debate) among a community of interpreters. Thus low inter-rater agreement may actually signal a more insightful assessment, especially if it leads to consensus, negotiation, or compromise (see Paulson and Paulson, 1991; Wolf et al., 1991).

There are many examples of this kind of assessment in practice. Moss (1994) uses the example of the way hiring decisions are made in higher education. Candidates for positions often assemble collections of their work that they think best document what they can bring to a position. Search committee members are selected not because they share a common, well trained perspective, but because they represent a broad area of expertise and interest. They do not agree to a common set of criteria or standards. Rather, they represent a collective expertise. Each member examines the full set of materials and together they make an integrative judgment about the candidate following negotiation and compromise. Moss suggests it would be unfair to seek only the same materials from each candidate and set the same judgment criteria to cover all, concluding ". . . permitting those assessed to choose products that best represent their strengths and interests may, in some circumstances, enhance not only validity but also fairness" (Moss, 1994, p. 8).

Ways Portfolio Assessment Differs from Other Kinds of Assessment

When we began working with portfolios, we were initially attracted to them as an assessment alternative to standardized tests. Like many other educators, we were concerned with the contrived and overly simplified way that standardized achievement tests defined and quantified learning. Our concerns were less with the assessment aspects of achievement testing than with the effects that achievement testing [has] on the quality of instruction. Resnick and Resnick (1992) have documented the effects of high stakes achievement testing on what and how things are taught in the classroom. Mary Lee Smith (1991) observed evidence of achievement testing leading to what she calls *multiple choice teaching.* Moss points a finger more directly at the assessment model used in constructing tests, noting that,

> The strength in the portfolio concept was that it . . . included assessment as one, but only one feature.

"Current conceptions of reliability and validity in educational measurement constrain the kinds of assessment practices that are likely to find favor, and these in turn constrain educational opportunities for teachers and students" (1994, p. 10). Even performance tests contain elements that impose the test writer's constructs on the student. Elsewhere (Paulson and Paulson, 1991), we have expressed concern that efforts to attain reliability through high inter-rater agreement may actually degrade the quality of assessment (see also Wolf et al., 1991).

As soon as we began to think about portfolios, however, it became clear that they were much more than merely an assessment device. The strength in the portfolio concept was that it was a total learning environment that included assessment as one, but only one feature, albeit a central one. Within the context of a student portfolio, instruction and assessment coexisted in an extremely compatible manner.

Briefly put, we saw the educational power of portfolios in their traditional context of the arts as opposed to the traditional context of educational assessment. Educational assessment invariably involved testing students and having other people make meaning of student performance. Remember Hansen's (1993) definition: tests are representational techniques that are externally imposed and constrained. But the kind of assessment observed in the context of portfolios involved creating, reflecting on, and evaluating meaning—where all stakeholders make meaning and the student changes the meaning while it's in the making!

While many educators would agree that it is important to teach students to be their own assessors, to us portfolio assessment offered an avenue to bring students into the very center of the assessment process. Thus, portfolio assessment became the model for a new kind of classroom assessment in which the student became a full stakeholder in the assessment process itself. In this model, the student assumes a leading role in the categories of activity that Robert Stake (1967) listed in his assessment model: setting the purpose, choosing goals, setting standards, collecting data, and interpreting the results. In "Sarah's Portfolio" (Paulson, Paulson, and Frazier, in press), we describe a portfolio used in this way.

CONCLUSIONS

How, the positivist tradition asks, can you have a highly individual document that will provide information that can be aggregated? Their answer is that you cannot, that [it] is necessary to impose standardization (i.e., make portfolios representational and imposed—a *test* according to Hansen's definition). Testing is "top-down"—something done to someone by another. But portfolios are "bottom-up"—reflecting the desire of someone to communicate documentable information. By imposing standardization, you destroy the individuality of the portfolio, thus subverting the very process you are trying to promote. While the standardization may have created something interesting and even useful for the purposes of assessment, that thing is not a portfolio and cannot be expected to yield the benefits of the portfolio as a method of encouraging self-directed learning (Paulson, Paulson, and Meyer, 1991). At best, you produce only a complex performance assessment.

> Portfolios are "bottom-up"— reflecting the desire of someone to communicate documentable information.

But in creating a complex performance assessment, you strip the portfolio of one of its major instructional benefits. The portfolio is a way of including students in the assessment process. It is a place where it is perfectly legitimate for the student to deliberately try to influence others' beliefs in what they know. The portfolio is a way of changing the relationship between the student and the assessment process itself—to turn it upside down to make the student a full and active partner in his or her own learning and the assessment thereof, including the design of the assessments that determine the standards and judgments that are reached.

Portfolio assessment is much better suited to the constructivist (hermeneutic) than it is [to] the positivist (psychometric) model. The positivist model requires outcomes to be specified in advance, while in portfolio assessment, outcomes, while guided by general purposes, both emerge and are redefined during the instructional process. Just as there are no two students the same, neither are there two portfolios the same, or outcomes the same. A strength of the hermeneutic model is its ability to support synthesis, to reassemble what analysis takes apart. The positivist model supports analysis much better than it handles synthesis. Portfolios are, by their nature, holistic. They are more than the sum of the parts. Efforts to apply the positivist model to portfolios invariably impose meanings on the portfolio that are different from those created by the learner.

As we followed the two projects, we see portfolios in the two projects as fitting two very different paradigms. The Atlanta, Georgia, project is concerned with large-scale evaluation and became more and more like externally administered collections of performance assessments. Yet portfolios from that project are also more amenable to psychometric analysis in the positivist paradigm. At the same time, we see the portfolios from Wyoming, Michigan, becoming more student-directed collections of authentic learning. They are more amenable to hermeneutic assessment consistent with the constructivist paradigm but have not been used this way in a large-scale assessment project. While several large-scale assessment projects employ methods similar to the Atlanta project (e.g., projects in Vermont and Oregon), we have yet to see large-scale projects in which individual portfolios are evaluated using constructivist assumptions.

NOTES

1. Trevisan, Paulson, and Weaver (in preparation) used one of the activities, a rating of students' ability to make scientific observations, to compare two contrasting third grade science curricula and found it an efficient and sound performance assessment.
2. We apply her discussion of hermeneutic (interpretive) philosophy to "constructivism."
3. Shavelson et al. (1993) conducted a generalizability study looking at sources of error in many kinds of performance assessments. They discov-

ered that inter-rater agreement tended to be a negligible source of error but that error associated with task was considerable in itself and when it interacted with persons (students). They conclude, "In the end, task sampling variability appears to be a fact, not an artifact" (p. 23), underlining the blurring distinction between reliability and validity in performance assessment. The implications when the psychometric model is used can be summed as, "Regardless of subject matter (math or science), domain (education or job performance), or level of analysis (individual or school), large numbers of tasks are needed to get a generalizable measure of performance" (p. 22).

REFERENCES

Calfee, R., and Perfumo, P. (1993). Student portfolios: Opportunities for a revolution in assessment. *Journal of Reading, 36*(7), 532–37.

Deming, W. E. (1986). *Out of the crisis.* Cambridge, MA: MIT, Center for Advanced Engineering Study.

Gitlow, H. S., and Gitlow, S. J. (1987). *The Deming guide to quality and competitive position.* Englewood Cliffs, NJ: Prentice Hall.

Guba, E., and Lincoln, Y. (1989). *Fourth generation evaluation.* Newbury Park: Sage.

Hansen, F. A. (1993). *Testing testing: Social consequences of an examined life.* Berkeley: University of California Press.

Jorgensen, M. (1994). Alternative assessment from the perspective of six different school systems—An experiment in consensus building. Paper presented at a meeting of the American Educational Research Association in New Orleans.

Jorgensen, M. (1993). Authentic assessment for multiple users. Paper presented to the National Association for Research in Science Teaching and available from Educational Testing Service, 1979 Lakeside Pkwy, Suite 400, Atlanta, GA 30084.

Koretz, D., Stecher, B., and Diebert, E. (1992). *The Vermont portfolio assessment program: Interim report on the implementation and impact, 1991–92 school year* (CSE Technical Report 350). Los Angeles: UCLA, Center for the Study of Evaluation.

Koretz, D., McCaffery, D., Klein, S., Bell, R., and Stecher, B. (1993). *The reliability of scores from the 1992 Vermont portfolio assessment program* (CSE Technical Report 355). Los Angeles: UCLA, Center for the Study of Evaluation.

Lincoln, Y. E., and Guba, E. G. (1985). *Naturalistic inquiry.* Beverly Hills: Sage.

Moss, P. A. (1994). Can there be validity without reliability? *Educational Researcher, 23*(2), 5–12.

Paulson, F. L. (1993). Bridging the gap: Applying Deming's "quality by design" to portfolios. Keynote address, Portfolio Conference in the Heartland, sponsored by Heartland AEA, Johnston, Iowa, April 1993. (Available from ERIC Document Reproduction Service).

Paulson, F. L., and Paulson, P. R. (in press). Four varieties of self-reflection. In K. Yancey (Ed.), *Portfolios: Voices from the field.* Urbana, IL: NCTE.

Paulson, F. L., and Paulson, P. R. (1991, April). The ins and outs of using portfolios to assess performance (Revised). In *Measurement Issues in Performance Assessment,* a symposium conducted by the National Council on Measurement in Education, Chicago. (ERIC Document Reproduction Service No. ED 334 250).

Paulson, F. L., and Paulson, P. R. (1990, August). How do portfolios measure up? A cognitive model for assessing portfolios. Paper presented at a conference Aggregating Portfolio Data sponsored by the Northwest Evaluation Association, Union, WA. (ERIC Document Reproduction Service No. ED 324 329).

Paulson, F. L., Paulson, P. R., and Meyer, C. A. (1991, February). What makes a portfolio a portfolio? *Educational Leadership, 46*(6), 60–63.

Paulson, P. R., Paulson, F. L., and Frazier, D. F. (in press). Sarah's portfolio. In K. Yancey (Ed.), *Portfolios: Voices from the field.* Urbana, IL: NCTE.

Paulson, P. R., and Paulson, F. L. (1991). Portfolios: Stories of knowing. In P. H. Dreyer (Ed.), *Claremont reading conference 55th yearbook 1991. Knowing: The power of stories* (pp. 294–303). Claremont, CA: Center for Development Studies of the Claremont Graduate School.

Resnick, L. B., and Resnick, D. P. (1992). Assessing the thinking curriculum: New tools for educational reform. In B. R. Gifford and M. C. O'Connor (Eds.), *Changing Assessments: Alternative views of aptitude, achievement and instruction.* Boston: Klewer.

Rutlin, A. (personal communication). For information, contact Wyoming Public Schools, 3575 Gladiola St. S. W., Wyoming, MI 49504.

Smith, M. L. (1991). Put to the test: The effects of external testing on teachers. *Educational Researcher, 20*(5), 8–11.

Suen, H. K., and Davey, B. (1990). Potential theoretical and practical pitfalls and cautions of the performance assessment design. Paper read at the annual meeting of the American Educational Research Association, Boston, MA.

Trevisan, M., Paulson, F. L., and Weaver, K. (in preparation). *An evaluation of a laser-disk science curriculum.* Gresham, OR: Gresham School District.

Viechnicki, K. J., Rohrer, J., Ambrose, R., and Barbour, N. (1992, April). The impact of portfolio assessment on teacher's classroom activities. Paper presented at the annual meeting of the American Educational Research Association in San Francisco.

Weiss, C. (1973). Where politics and evaluation research meet. *Evaluation, 1,* 37–45.

Wolf, D., Bixby, J., Glenn, J., and Gardner, H. (1991). To use their minds well: Investigating new forms of student assessment. In G. Grant (Ed.), *Review of research in education.* Vol. 17. Washington, DC: American Educational Research Association.

Wyoming Public Schools (undated, ca. 1993). PEP Talk: Portfolio exhibit planner: Secondary edition, and PEP Talk: Portfolio exhibit planner: Primary edition. Wyoming Public Schools, 3575 Gladiola St. S.W., Wyoming, MI 49509.

Portfolio Assessment

by Susan Black

Along with book bags and lunch boxes, many students now tote something new to school—portfolios of their work. The use of portfolios is becoming increasingly popular in U.S. schools as teachers look for alternatives to traditional tests to measure student progress. But so new is the portfolio concept that there isn't yet much research to guide educators in setting up new systems. And that should signal a go-slow approach.

In fact, one recent research report from the RAND Corp., evaluating Vermont's portfolio assessment program, points to some serious problems with portfolios that should serve, according to report author Daniel Koretz, as a "warning call for people to be a little more cautious."

> **Researchers have long noted that traditional tests, standardized or otherwise, have clear limitations.**

Portfolios appeal to educators for good reason, though. Researchers have long noted that traditional tests, standardized or otherwise, have clear limitations. According to Joan L. Herman and S. Golan, for example, the content of the tests too often determines what is taught. These researchers (along with many others) find that tests "narrow the curriculum" to basic skills rather than higher-order thinking skills. Another researcher, Lorrie Shepard, reports that even when students do well on tests (often because teachers "teach to the test"), it doesn't mean they've learned anything valuable. Most likely, Shepard says, what they've learned is to take tests well.

From *The Executive Educator,* vol. 15, no. 1, February 1993, pp. 28–31. © 1993 by the National School Boards Association. Reprinted with permission.

Many teachers, for their part, maintain there's little match between what they teach and what tests measure. Teachers who stretch children's minds beyond simple memorization and who emphasize group problem solving and cooperative learning protest that standardized tests don't reflect their students' real knowledge and abilities.

Using portfolios without a clear plan can lead to misunderstandings with parents, administrators, and students.

Portfolios are one answer in the search for alternative ways to assess students' performance. Portfolios are supposed to represent what students know—to show, over time and in a variety of ways, the depth, breadth, and development of student's abilities, according to researchers Lorraine Valdez Pierce and J. Michael O'Malley.

But as any teacher who's tried portfolios will attest, deciding to use them is the easy part; it's much harder to ensure portfolios accurately record and measure student performance. Some state education departments and research labs do offer workshops and booklets on portfolio assessment. But teachers usually find it's best to experiment and develop their own strategies to fit their subject areas and their classrooms. The work of Ohio State University researcher Robert Tierney and his public school teacher colleagues encourages teachers along those lines.

But even under supportive circumstances, the change from traditional testing to portfolios isn't always easy. Judith Arter, a researcher with the Northwest Regional Educational Laboratory, says few teachers who are excited about the possibilities of using portfolios have worked out exactly what they mean by portfolios or how they should be used. And, says Arter, most teachers haven't anticipated or addressed the fallout issues that can accompany portfolio assessments.

Using portfolios without a clear plan can lead to misunderstandings with parents, administrators, and students. Teachers might also find some tasks bewildering, such as setting acceptable standards for student work, coordinating assessments with grading requirements, and storing archives. If teachers feel overwhelmed with the planning details, they might forsake their

Why Use Portfolios?

Here are some reasons to use portfolios, as set down by English and language arts teachers in California. These reasons are excerpted from *Testing for Learning*, by Ruth Mitchell, and adapted from *Portfolio News*, published by Portfolio Assessment Clearinghouse, c/o San Dieguito Union High School District, Encinitas, California.

1. **As a teaching tool**
   — to provide students ownership, motivation, a sense of accomplishment, and participation
   — to involve students in a process of self-evaluation
   — to help students and teachers set goals
   — to build in time for reflection about students' accomplishments
   — to aid in parent conferences

2. **Professional development of teachers**
   — to study curriculum and effective teaching practices
   — to allow for better staff communication
   — to reduce the paper load
   — to identify school strengths and needs for improvement
   — to build a sequence in writing instruction

3. **Assessment**
   — to serve as an alternative to standardized testing
   — to serve as a college application and high school placement vehicle
   — to replace competency exams
   — to serve as a grade of end-of-year culminating activity
   — to provide program evaluation
   — to supplement or substitute for state assessment tests

4. **Research**
   — to examine growth over time and progress in students' writing
   — to look at the revision process

good intentions. And if that happens, student portfolios might end up in the circular file.

THE VERMONT EXPERIENCE

In one of the best known portfolio programs, Vermont teachers helped the state department of education design a statewide system of portfolio assessment as one way of evaluating the results of a new writing program. The portfolios are now used in grades four and eight, with grade 11 to be added soon. A typical Vermont fourth-grader's portfolio contains these pieces: (1) a table of contents listing the pieces the student has selected; (2) the best pieces of writing as chosen by the student; (3) a letter—written by the student to the teacher and other reviewers—about the best piece, explaining why the student chose it and the process used to produce the final draft; (4) a poem, short story, play, or personal narrative; (5) a personal response to an event, program, or item of interest; and (6) a prose piece from any subject area other than English or language arts.

Vermont, which also uses portfolios to evaluate students' math progress, is a pioneer in implementing the approach, beginning in 1988. But the state is also a pioneer in coming face-to-face with the problems associated with portfolios. The evaluation by the RAND Corp., released in December, showed rater reliability—that is, the odds that two different teachers would rate a portfolio the same way—to be very low. The recommendations put forth in the report include improving training for teachers in how to score portfolios accurately and making changes in the scoring system itself, which the report suggests might be too complex. The report's author, Daniel Koretz, says Vermont is actively looking at instituting some of the changes and that RAND will continue its evaluation.

Koretz, a resident scholar at RAND, says those who begin using portfolios often want to accomplish two things: Improve what goes in the classroom, and find a good assessment tool. But, he says, those two goals can be at odds with each other. Improving what goes on in the classroom often means broadly training every teacher in rating student work. Assessing students accurately, on the other hand, could well require training only a small number of teachers at a time, but training them carefully and thoroughly.

The question that needs to be addressed, Koretz says, "is how to compromise between a powerful educational intervention and a decent assessment program."

Koretz also says it's important for school districts that opt for portfolio assessment to put in place a means for assessing the program. "People ought to have realistic expectations about how quickly [implementing a portfolio system] can be done and how it will come out the first time," he says. "A lot of people around the country have unrealistic expectations."

> It's important for school districts that opt for portfolio assessment to put in place a means for assessing the program.

MAKING WAY FOR PORTFOLIOS

Before moving toward the use of portfolios, other researchers agree, teachers must first think through their reasons for using this alternative assessment approach. Do they want to improve curriculum and teaching, or to assess student work—or perhaps both?

Teachers also must define exactly what they mean by portfolio as "a purposeful collection of student work that exhibits to the student and others effort, progress, or achievement in a given area or areas." F. Leon Paulson and Pearl R. Paulson emphasize process over product in their definition: "A portfolio is a carefully crafted portrait of what someone knows or can do." Teachers might find someone else's definition suitable, or they might choose to write their own.

Then there are the nitty-gritty decisions. What should be included in a portfolio? Who should select the contents? Should a portfolio reflect only a student's best work, or should it represent a spectrum of accomplishments and efforts? Should bulky items (such as science projects) be considered? What should the school keep for its permanent records? How should teachers communicate students' achievement to parents? How should teachers evaluate portfolios? What other kinds of assessment should be used, if any?

Answers to some of these questions can be found in research. Judith Arter notes that portfolio contents should be chosen according to their purpose. She finds that, in general, teachers either require certain items from each student or, with students, choose samples of work that reflect growth and development in a specific subject area.

F. Leon Paulson and Pearl R. Paulson find portfolios should be more than just collections of students' work. Portfolios, they say, ought to include students' narratives about how they produced the contents and about what they learned. Students' written reflections about their learning might be among the most valuable pieces in the portfolios, these researchers say.

The Paulsons maintain that "students own their portfolios," so they—not teachers—should create their collections and review their selections. They suggest that portfolios should tell a students' story, and anything that helps that story could be included—classroom assignments, finished or rough drafts, work students develop specifically for the portfolio to show their interests and abilities, self-reflections, and observations and comments by teachers or parents.

In her report, Sharon Althouse provides diagrams to guide teachers, students, and parents as they choose items for students' reading and writing portfolios. (Althouse's study found that teachers and students most often selected *writing* samples for portfolios.)

California math teacher Pam Knight encourages her algebra students to choose from their semester's worth of classwork and homework to construct well-balanced portfolios. Knight's students are likely to include long-term projects, daily notes, journal entries about difficult test problems, scale drawings, best and worst tests, and homework samples.

In some remedial programs, students design portfolios that align with their individual education plans. In Pennsylvania's Eastern Lancaster County School District, for example, teachers first identify two or three goals for each student in Chapter 1 reading and math. (Students may add goals of their own.) Portfolios are likely to include written compositions, records of books read, examples of drafts and revisions of written work, samples of math processes and problems, and original math story problems.

Teachers and researchers also report successful ventures using portfolios with high school science and social studies students. Missouri teachers use computer portfolios to capture their fifth-graders' reading progress. In Wyoming, elementary students use laser disk technology to record their verbal ability, physical accomplishments, artistic achievement, and self-assurance. Lorraine Valdez Pierce and J. Michael O'Malley describe how elementary and middle school students learning English as a second language use portfolios to show oral language and reading skills.

OTHER CONCERNS

Time and grades are among the other issues to consider before going ahead with portfolios. Managing portfolios takes time, that precious classroom commodity. But, researchers report, teachers who change from traditional assessment to portfolio assessment are more likely to manage their time without frustration if they change teaching styles at the same time. Rather than continuously assigning and grading workbook lessons, teachers

> **Managing portfolios takes time, that precious classroom commodity.**

should prompt students to learn through writing and exchanging ideas. Teachers can more efficiently and effectively guide instruction through cooperative learning groups. And teachers should hold conferences with their students to reinforce and motivate their learning and, when necessary, to reteach prerequisite skills.

Then there's the sticky issue of grades. How can teachers assign unit grades or report card grades (usually required by the district office, and perhaps by the state education department) when they're assessing students' portfolios for effort, progress, and insight as well for as specific achievement? Some districts are experimenting with new kinds of report cards—using checklists and narratives, for example—that more closely reflect their new assessments.

It's imperative that teachers inform and educate students and parents about new grading systems. Even when they're pleased with their portfolios and their teachers' comments, some students demand familiar letter grades—especially when they're accustomed to earning A's and B's. Sometimes parents give portfolio assessment systems cool receptions because they don't understand the new evaluation reports. They might prefer their children's report card to look just like the ones they used to bring home from school.

It's important to discuss a new portfolio assessment system with students and parents. In Sharon Althouse's Pennsylvania pilot project, students doubted their parents would understand the portfolios, even when teachers enclosed letters explaining the new assessment plan. And, Althouse reports, students often changed the contents of their portfolios when they knew their parents would examine their selections. Though parents expressed appreciation and approval of the portfolio system, they provided skimpy answers or no answers at all to a short survey about the new method.

> It's important to discuss a new portfolio assessment system with students and parents.

Finally, other considerations might arise. In high schools, students and parents might object to portfolio assessment on the grounds that college admissions offices require grades and class rankings. And at any grade level, serious questions remain about the objectivity of portfolio assessment. Any program of portfolio assessment must address the possibility that assessments might be biased on the basis of race, sex, or cultural orientation or overly generous so as to bolster students' self-esteem.

A SUCCESSFUL START

If your school or school district is considering using portfolio assessments, what can you do to help the new approach succeed? You can begin by setting agendas for staff planning and staff development. The Northwest Regional Educational Laboratory (NWREL) proposes tackling these topics: purpose, curriculum and instruction, content, assessment, management and logistics, and staff development. Specific questions to discuss, NWREL researchers say, include: What are the purposes for using portfolios? How will portfolios reflect the school's curriculum? How must instruction change to support portfolio assessments? What is acceptable in a student portfolio? Who owns the portfolio, and who chooses the contents? What other types of student assessment will the school use? How will portfolio assessments be coordinated among grade levels? How will assessments be communicated to parents?

You need to invest time and effort helping teachers *before* they begin using portfolio assessments, but you also need to offer support to teachers who might encounter problems *after* they've started up with their new system. Peer coaching—pairing teachers who are reluctant or uneasy about using student portfolios with teachers who easily are incorporating the new method in their classrooms—might help teachers who want to throw in the towel and return to traditional testing alone. Workshops at which teachers examine models and then work out their own plans can also help get portfolio assessments off to a smooth start.

It's a long and often rocky road to institutionalize any innovation in education. Even when teachers are eager to accept a new plan, you can bet the process will be one of fits and starts. When it comes to developing portfolio assessments, you'll need to encourage teachers not to give up when they face difficult issues. But you'll also have to remind them—and yourself—to go slow with this new approach to assessment.

REFERENCES

Alexander, L., et. al. "The Nation's Report Card: Improving the Assessment of Student Achievement." Cambridge, Mass.: National Academy of Education. 1987.

Althouse, S. M. "A Pilot Project Using Portfolios to Document Progress in the School Program." Paper presented at the annual meeting of the International Reading Association. May 1991.

Arter, J. "Curriculum-Referenced Test Development Workshop Theory: Using Portfolios in Instruction and Assessment." Portland, Ore.: Northwest Regional Educational Laboratory. Nov. 1990. ERIC Document No. ED 335 364.

Ballard, L. "Portfolios and Self-Assessment." *English Journal,* Feb. 1992, 81, 46–48.

Cooper, W., and Brown, B.J. "Using Portfolios to Empower Student Writers." *English Journal,* Feb. 1992, 81, 40–45.

Herbert, E.A. "Portfolios Invite Reflection—from Students and Staff." *Educational Leadership,* May 1992, 58–61.

Herman, J.L. "What Research Tells Us about Good Assessment." *Educational Leadership,* May 1992, 74–78.

Herter, R.J. "Writing Portfolios: Alternatives to Testing." *English Journal,* Jan. 1991, 90–91.

Hetterscheidt, J., et al. "Using the Computer as a Reading Portfolio." *Educational Leadership,* May 1992, 73.

Knight, P. "How I Use Portfolios in Mathematics." *Educational Leadership,* May 1992, 71–72.

Koretz, D., et al. *The Reliability of Scores from the 1992 Vermont Portfolio Assessment Program: Interim Report.* Washington, D.C.: RAND Institute on Education and Training, Dec. 1992.

Mitchell, R. *Testing for Learning.* New York: The Free Press (Macmillan, Inc.), 1992.

New York State United Teachers. "Multiple Choices: Reforming Student Testing in New York State. A Report of the NYSUT Task Force in Student Assessment." Jan. 1991.

Paulson, F.L., and Paulson, P.R. "The Ins and Outs of Using Portfolios to Assess Performance (Revised)." Expanded paper presented at the joint annual meeting of the National Council of Measurement in Education, April 1991.

Paulson, F.L., and Paulson, P.R. "The Making of a Portfolio." Prepublished Draft. Feb. 1991, 1–11.

Shepard, L. "Will National Tests Improve Student Learning?" *Phi Delta Kappan,* Nov. 1991, 232–38.

Tierney, R.J., Carter, M.A., and Desai, L.E. *Portfolio Assessment in the Reading-Writing Classroom.* Norwood, Mass.: Christopher-Gordon Publishers, Inc., 1991.

Valencia, S.W. "Alternative Assessment: Separating the Wheat from the Chaff." *The Reading Teacher,* 1990, 43, 60–61.

Wiggins, G. "The Case for Authentic Assessment." ERIC Clearinghouse on Tests, Measurement, and Evaluation, Dec. 1990.

Yunginger-Gehman, J. "A Pilot Project for Portfolio Assessment in a Chapter 1 Program." Paper presented at the Annual Meeting of the International Reading Association, May 1991.

Section 2

The Mission: Using Portfolios

To travel hopefully is a better thing than to arrive.—Robert Louis Stevenson

Once a decision is made to use portfolios, the teacher must then learn how to use them. This second section focuses on the practicalities of actually initiating and implementing portfolios as part of the assessment strategy in the classroom. Presented in six content-rich discussions, all phases of developing portfolios are illuminated, including initial decisions, implementation ideas, and the role of technology. The six articles appearing here provide a cursory look at the nitty-gritty aspects of putting portfolio assessment in place in the classroom.

The opening article by Judith Fueyo poses a thought-provoking question that cuts to the heart of portfolio development: What do we really care about? In this interesting discussion of the issues that surround our true purposes for using portfolios, the author explores the idea of "the spirit of portfolios" and portfolios as rites of passage.

In another piece, Susan Mandel Glazer, Katrin-Kaja Rooman, and Kristine Luberto suggest that the search for user-friendly portfolios begins with an agreed-upon agenda, an understanding of tools for assessment such as benchmarks, a well-articulated focus, and practical ideas for the practitioner that range from portfolio models to Post-it note comments to "proud" portfolios. Based on the actual development of portfolios as an ongoing part of assessment by two teachers, the discussion is perky, practical, and to the point.

F. Leon Paulson, Pearl R. Paulson, and Carol A. Meyer provide insight into the portfolio process in an article entitled "What Makes a Portfolio a Portfolio?" The authors skillfully outline eight guidelines that help educators encourage self-directed learning through the use of portfolios. Among other ideas, they stress the need for the end product to demonstrate self-reflection; artifacts done by students, not to students; evidence of progress toward student-selected goals; and illustrations of student growth and development. They conclude with an answer to their original question, "When is a portfolio a portfolio?," by stating that it is when a portfolio provides a complete and comprehensive view of student performance in context, when students participate in the process, and when it provides a forum for students to become self-directed learners.

Inspired by vignettes depicting actual applications of portfolio assessment throughout the United States and Canada, Robin Fogarty, Kay Burke, and Susan Belgrad delineate a ten-step process for the development of student portfolios. Stressing the steps of collecting, selecting, and reflecting as the primary concerns, the authors also illustrate how the process can be easily enhanced with additional phases. These steps might include projecting purposes, interjecting new artifacts, connecting with others in conferences, and inspecting and perfecting through performance assessment rubrics.

With a focus on portfolios as a way to sample student work and in the process encourage students to assess their own work, Dennie Palmer Wolf also makes the point that portfolios provide a format for teachers to view their accomplishments in teaching as well. The article spells out the value of students' showcasing a biography of a work, a range of various kinds of work, and work that includes student reflections.

This section concludes with two timely and informative articles that provide insight into the issue of how technology impacts on the implementation of student portfolios in the classroom. The article by Christopher Moersch and Louis M. Fisher III focuses on some pivotal questions that surround the use of electronic portfolios. The authors deal not only with what should be included, but also with how the work samples get into the computer and how to reduce entry time. In addition, they suggest available tools that help teachers use the electronic process.

Helen C. Barrett, in a complementary article, presents a particularly useful discussion on technology-supported assessment portfolios from the students' view. In this highly practical piece, the author specifically mentions new software that allows students to document their education in text, images, and sound. The author further suggests that teachers can start simply, by storing student files on floppy disks or hard disks and keeping student performances on videotape. From these easy-to-use beginnings, teachers and students advance as the software and hardware become accessible in their schools. The inclusion of these two essays is an intentional signal to readers that technology plays a role in the implementation of portfolios and that that role is more than likely to become increasingly important.

"What Do You Really Care about Here?": Portfolios as Rites of Passage

by Judith Fueyo

THE SEDUCTION
Outside my office in the College of Education, where the majority of instructors and professors in language and literacy use portfolios as key elements of student evaluation, the hallway is banked by orphaned portfolios. Nightly, Sue, the cleaning lady, dodges the portfolio piles, trying to dust-mop the floor. Nightly, as I leave, the ghosts of past students titter between the covers of these purportedly soul-felt reflections on their literacy growth.

Across town, my friend Jocelyn, whose titles include Coordinator of K–12 Reading and K–6 Language Arts/Social Studies, fields calls from anxious third- and sixth-grade teachers needing to know what to do with "all this stuff." They fall heir, respectively, to portfolios of work spanning Grades K–2 and Grades 3–6 for each child. They ask, "At what point does it become too much? How much do my kids add this year?"

"I don't know. You'll tell me at the end of next year. We are in the driver's seat. All we've been asked to do so far is 'devise portfolios,'" Jocelyn coaches. "I don't want to define. I want you to play around with them. Hopefully, whatever we devise, folks will value them and keep them."

That's what I hoped for, too. Still, if my students' portfolios appeared "soul-felt," why are they often abandoned, these oft-three-inch-thick literate histories? If so attuned to literate

From *Language Arts,* vol. 71, no. 6, October 1994, pp. 404–10. © 1994 by the National Council of Teachers of English. Reprinted with permission.

growth, why do faculty dread the days of judgment and sit-ins that follow due dates? Why the confessions that in a pinch we've handed in grades before we've plowed through all the piles? Why, even, the whispered threat by a colleague only doors away that she's considering "an objective midterm"? Why, some 4 years and nearly 500 student portfolios later, do I feel as if I've fallen out of love? The initial seduction of the portfolio has cooled down for me.

Sure, I squatted on dusty floors at NCTE's portfolio sessions, eagerly seeking guidance from portfolio proponents. I bought the books and tapes, attended workshops, and even gave some workshops. In my vita I claim to "investigate portfolios as congruent for literacy evaluation." At this writing, I'm developing a new graduate course called "Investigating Portfolios," and Jocelyn is urging district teachers to take it. It's time I figured this out.

> I've wept over portfolios that were extremely personal or insightful, or extremely lousy.

Like the early computers that filled whole rooms, writing portfolios glut my already cramped office. I have a total of only 60 or so students at a time, and still I joke about bringing in an air mattress so I can stay nights to get through their portfolios and give them meaningful responses. I've wept over portfolios that were extremely personal or insightful, or extremely lousy. I've developed several of my own and believed I had to develop yet another version with each of my classes.

So, after such a committed relationship, do I now end it? Yes and no. I needed portfolios to get from where I was to where I am now to where I need to go next. Portfolios were a rite of passage necessary to free me from less authentic assessment. And because my experience was and remains valuable, I'll support Jocelyn and her teachers in their journey and expect to learn more of what portfolios might become from them.

THE MAKING OF A NEW CULTURE
Historically, literacy assessment has been driven by a hierarchy of external standards and authorities that placed the learner at the bottom (Rose, 1989). Portfolio assessment—if conception

and execution remained with learners, be they individual students, teachers, schools, or whole districts—fundamentally upended this hierarchy. Up until process writing entered the scene during the 1970s and 1980s—and the subsequent, larger undertaking "whole language" followed—assessment packages generally came from out of town, from the very companies whose materials drove the literacy curriculum (Shannon, 1994). Only in the last 15 years have teachers, districts, and even states looked to publishers outside the basal circuit for leadership in designing their own literacy curricula and literacy assessment.

By examining such publishers' offerings over the last 10 years, the themes that have dominated the literacy landscape, especially writing, emerge. For example, the early 80s' publications celebrated *that* children could write, what this process looked/sounded like, and how to set up the classroom to enable writing. The mid-80s focused on reading-writing connections and more in-depth studies of teaching writing, while the late 80s invested writing with power for "creating and refining one's own meaning, not simply a way of recording and reporting someone else's" (1988 Heinemann Boynton/Cook Catalogue, p. 12). Writing was no longer just the end product of thinking or doing research; it was generative along the way—across the curriculum.

Texts explicitly designed to evaluate literacy growth in ways better suited to whole language or process teaching began appearing only within the last 6 years, and the notion of portfolio assessment is even more recent. In one of these texts, *Portfolio Portraits,* Donald Graves (1992) cautions: "We need to explore the many uses of portfolios for at least another five years, and perhaps indefinitely. Without careful exploration, portfolio use is doomed to failure. They will be too quickly tried, found wanting, and just as quickly abandoned" (p. 1). I have no problem with abandonment, however, if it's done after a process of discernment involving students, teachers, parents, and people like Jocelyn. Tom Romano (1992) admits: "When you get right down to it, it's not the portfolio that matters most…[but] the *process*" (p. 157). That process is what I'd call "the spirit of portfolios"; that is what I want to retain in whatever assessment repertoire I use.

THE SPIRIT OF PORTFOLIO

"It's you I like, not the clothes you wear." Can you still hear Mr. Rogers reminding children it's their essence as human beings he likes and not their possessions? Likewise, it's the spirit of the literacy portfolio I like and am committed to, not its trappings. That spirit of portfolio honors whole human beings, not parts; honors wholeness of language, not just pieces; honors intentions and processes, not just products; honors habits of mind, artistic vision, initiative, persistence, multiple media for communication, reflection, and self-evaluation. That spirit of portfolio essentially gives me and my students responsibility for shaping literacy assessment to fit lives in and out of school. The terms "empowerment," "independence," and "care" characterize that spirit for Tierney, Carter, and Desai (1991). Their text was one of the first whole texts to offer an historical, conceptual, and useful, though overly specific, vision of portfolios.

> It's the spirit of the literacy portfolio I like and am committed to, not its trappings.

In my experience, however, routinely requiring students to mount such productions was beginning to be too much—both in course time and emphasis. The proverbial assessment tail was wagging the curricular dog. Of our 15-week semester in a language arts course based on the writing workshop, about one-fourth was spent on evaluation in general, and much of that on the development of our own writing portfolios. Early in the course I would introduce portfolios as an option to reflect growth during the semester. I'd wheel in a cartload of abandoned portfolios so these students could become familiar with the form. These portfolios span my own teaching growth because they cover 4 years' courses and more years' development of my own thinking. For example, influenced by Donald Graves' early concepts of range, depth, and growth, portfolios from my early courses are fattest. At that time I invited students to reflect their writing selves both in and out of school, past, present, and future. Consequently, these portfolios frequently showcase writings from before kindergarten up through the present: delightful family treasures, but unwieldy, even inappropriate characterizations of what we were about. I'd overdone a good thing. Portfolios from recent courses reflect a more narrow focus to show development of professional and/or personal issues, or of genres. Regardless of the thematic focus, however, what remained constant was that most students learned to articulate their growth, to choose what they needed/wanted to learn next, and to reflect on the meaning of such self-determination.

Still, many portfolios represent hours that might have been better spent revising existing pieces. Although I stress the value of revision on an already "published" piece, few students take me up on it, perhaps due to time constraints, lack of interest, or the pressure to get a portfolio assembled. Frequently during co-evaluation of a portfolio (students self-evaluate, using some criteria we develop as a class and some that [are] unique), I'd wish I were reading a piece of their writing that they had revised, truly made better. I'd get the feeling I was reading last Friday's student newspaper: well-done stuff, but old news because we'd both seen it before. For students doing portfolios for the second time in as many semesters, the experience appeared forced. I longed for the good old days of the late 1980s when we were writing and reading more and collecting, selecting, and reflecting less. But, I questioned, Too much for whom?

In his book, *A Door Opens: Writing in Fifth Grade,* Jack Wilde (1993) states that "writing autobiographical stories to foster revision became an opportunity to look at product as well as process" (p. 20). How ironic that one would need to say that! However, in my writing workshops I, too, experienced much more student writing, but precious little that was excellent. I've sat on my hands to avoid handling a student's draft and held my tongue to let the writer lead the conference. Yes, indeed, I'm a facilitator. Of what? I suspected that in the interest of creating a low-risk environment, excellent writing took a beating. And the portfolios confirmed my suspicions with one critical addition: Now students were self-evaluating.

How could I merge humane attention to excellence and time/experience in self-evaluation? How could I regain a classroom culture that prizes writing and revision above all, that includes but does not dwell on assessment? Those texts that focus on crafting writing were the books that once fueled most of my lessons. Now, however, I flooded students with lessons on portfolio possibilities. Somewhere along the way, once I got the feel of classroom organization, I got sidetracked by the portfolio sirens promising that I could trim those fat student writing folders to manageable size and still have a life. It took me 8 years and many hours to learn that it wasn't the portfolio per se that transformed assessment: It was giving students more responsibility for naming and claiming their own growth, for reflecting on the word and the world.

> It wasn't the portfolio per se that transformed assessment: It was giving students more responsibility for naming and claiming their own growth.

So, once my seduction by portfolios cooled down, I rediscovered my true love, why I teach writing in the first place: to help students exploit the power of language, to gain more control of their lives. At the university level, the best way I know to do that is to create a culture of revision, where the artist labors willingly in the service of art. Bartholomae and Petrosky's (1986) *Facts, Artifacts and Counterfacts;* Shaughnessy's (1977) *Errors and Expectations;* Calkins and Harwayne's (1991) *Living between the Lines;* Murray's (1991) *The Craft of Revision;* Burroway's (1987) *Fiction Writing;* Pappas, Kiefer, and Levstik's (1990) *An Integrated Language Perspective in the Elementary School;* and the writing I do for courses I audit here in the English Department at Penn State once again dominate my mini-lessons. Hence, I no longer devote as much time to the broad assessment sweep at semester's end. Instead, we all construct verbal or nonverbal metaphors of our growth. (For more on metaphor, see Mem Fox's book, *Radical Reflections* [1993], and John Mayher's *Uncommon Sense* [1990].) In addition, we document one piece of writing as process and product. Finally, we self-evaluate both our metaphors and our written pieces, using unique and shared criteria.

This past semester, I spread my own metaphor-in-progress on the classroom floor for students to see, a literal tapestry of various threads to link all my writing selves—assistant professor, ex-high school teacher, mother, friend, daughter, reader, theater nut, student of fiction writing, and so on. I wanted them to see that my multiple, entwined reading/writing lives energized and informed each other. I lay these varied writing/reading texts along colored yarns, twisted and knotted them to make connections visible, and shared by metaphor orally, although much of it was still only notes sketched out on a napkin and books and writings stashed in a box. I wanted to make transparent my process of constructing an idiosyncratic literacy metaphor and sharing it in less that 5 minutes. Finally, I published a hard copy of my metaphor: a collage incorporating the yarns to connect readings, my writings, and brief written reflections to explain the connections and meanings. Students followed suit in metaphors that fit their own journeys.

The above assessment repertoire has been a long time coming. No doubt its form, too, will change but, I trust, not its spirit. Indeed, as I write this, I'm tinkering with syllabi to give more weight to collaborative multimedia projects that produce positive change outside the classroom. No doubt, too, across town Jocelyn's faculty will be tinkering with their assessment repertoires in fundamentally different ways in the future because they wrestled with portfolio assessment. The issue is not whether I or they keep portfolios; it is that each of us is for once "in the driver's seat."

AN ON-AGAIN-OFF-AGAIN RELATIONSHIP

To probe further the "spirit of portfolios," I surveyed practicing and preservice teachers in my literacy courses; most who had experienced portfolios passionately and articulately defended the process, but some who had never done portfolios lamented the missed opportunity. The most compelling argument for portfolios came from Mary Anne, a veteran high school English teacher. After listening to classmates' portfolio praises as well as my concerns, she said, "I hear you, Judy, but I cannot sympathize. Show me the classroom where kids are doing too much reflecting on their reading and writing at the expense of either. Reflection? What's that? And you expect me to add this to what I already have to teach? You've got to be kidding."

Putting aside students' possible ulterior motives for championing portfolios, I admitted ambivalence. How could my portfolio relationship have come to this—potentially transformative for students but disappointing for me? How could I underestimate what I ask teachers to do in their own classrooms—to invent environments and curricula to fit their students' lives here and now? How could I underestimate my challenge to them to discard institutionalized, packaged assessment deals? Indeed, how could I now underestimate the process I, too, had gone through?

Over the past several years, more certain of why old assessment routines didn't work, I developed more and more elaborate conceptions of portfolios. Pity the students who came to me at the height of the romance! It's little wonder some never picked up their portfolios; they're too heavy to lug home.

Still, most students did lug the things home. Many claim that the experience of self-evaluation is nothing less than transformative. Many celebrate the merger of their professional and personal selves for the first time inside an institution. Some admit that for the first time they understood revision only because they realized that to document the how's and why's of revision, they needed to revise! To document their decisions within the portfolio, they needed to make decisions!

> **Many claim that the experience of self-evaluation is nothing less than transformative.**

So, where am I now? I strongly urge those who have never constructed a portfolio to do so. For others, I'll continue to woo them with the joys of revision and invite them to design different assessment repertoires using, once again, unique and shared criteria. How I wish I could revise the grade I gave a student whose writing was excellent, but whose portfolio was miserable. He'd collected his best pieces, attached to them Post-its with minuscule critiques here and there (read, "for the teacher"), and dumped all into a manila folder. Clearly, for him, the portfolio experience was not educative in the Deweyian sense, but perfunctory. This student knew when his writing measured up to his standards, and he valued improving his writing and letting it speak for itself over documenting the improvement. I was reminded of my brief stint as a technical writer for an insurance company, where I had to document my work per 15-minute chunk. If only I could have called up an alter ego like Towanda in *Fried Green Tomatoes at the Whistle Stop Cafe* (Flagg, 1987), I would have recorded: "Three minutes spent recording 'three minutes,' you fools."

Still, for many students, the process of collecting, selecting, and reflecting is crucial. In *No Sense of Place,* Joshua Meyrowitz (1985) illustrates the ambivalent bound-aries of self-definition, especially of child-hood, in our media-saturated era. Experi-ences of childhood, community, even family are so mobile that new under-standing of "self" are ongoing. Portfolios, because they must be customized, and be-cause they demand we name the what's, how's, and why's of our reading/writing ventures, situate us, for one brief shining moment, in a time and place. Portfolios pow-erfully document our literate relationships—to classmates, emulated authors, favored genres, causes, themes, and curricu-lar and extracurricular concerns—and their meanings at certain junctures of our lives. I have long observed that inservice and preservice teachers in my teaching writing classes explore simi-lar themes and arrive at similar places by course's end. During the portfolio process, however, they see the journey.

> **Portfolios powerfully document our literate relationships and their meanings.**

Typically, the journey runs along three successive paths. On the first, teachers experience new respect for themselves as writers. On the second, many tackle tough issues such as di-vorce of parents or spouses, depression, gender issues, alcohol-ism, homesickness, moving, being dumped by boss or lover, and the like. On the third path, most turn their energies out-ward toward their present or future classrooms and their wider circles of influence. In other words, on a process level, writing in a community of writers is new and powerful. On a content level, confronting personal and professional issues in a public forum is powerful, too. These experiences then combine to help persons see themselves as active knowers and doers, and the portfolio process is likely to make all this even clearer.

Students' words from their portfolios speak best to illus-trate these three paths. Ruth, a primary grade teacher, included this in her portfolio introduction: "Always it was the secondary English teachers who knew terms like 'voice' and 'tone.' I never really got into that when I was in high school. But now, because I'm writing for myself for the first time in my life, I care and I get it." Don, a seasoned upper elementary teacher, introduced a section of original poetry in his portfolio with the following verse:

Too Late I Turned
The reading of verse is a puzzle that's worse
than the famous Gordian Knot.
How's it done? Can't be much fun
when your poet's license's expired.
You must be so nimble to catch the symbol
that infests those torturous plots,
It may be easy for you, but I haven't a clue
of the language that is required.
When I was a boy, we thought it a ploy
to deprive us of our manhood.
You would have to be kidding if you thought of us sitting
with that stuff made for a sissy.
We all dreaded the junk and were sure that it stunk
and spurned what we knew was no good.
We should rather be hung or over a cliff be flung
than to try something so prissy.
Those old days are gone and so is my frown
turned to'rd all that is poetic.
My trouble right now is that I don't know how
to battle this terrible shame.
This fine way of showing what inside is glowing
is lost to this ruing old tick,
So bloated with dust and gathering rust
of seeking naught but the plain.

He struggled to write poetry honestly for the first time and confront stereotypical gender demons throughout the workshop semester. Conceiving and executing his portfolio helped him to name and value his themes and purposes. Out of such experience grows a new power, a critical attitude that extends beyond the writing community. For example, Sarah, another elementary teacher, wrote and included the following in her portfolio:

> During my school career I have never been a die-hard school-lover. . . . I loved to play school; I could be in control. I didn't like to go to school where everyone else made decisions about me . . . . The most important discovery that I have made is that I do

not have to accept everything that is told to me. I am capable of making professional decisions. I need to take a step back and ask myself, Why am I doing this? and, Do I believe in it?

I am proud to say that last week when my supervisor observed me, I did my thing. I taught the way that I believed in and not necessarily the way I was told. When I had my conference, I explained it even further. I took ownership for my action and reasons.

A portfolio experience, then, can be critical for those of us who wish to teach literacy critically. We can't give what we don't have. As a consequence of assembling their work, naming their passions, then reflecting and evaluating the cumulative whole, many experience for the first time that outer circle of critical/metalanguage that James Gee (1987) insists is critical literacy, the literacy that questions how and to what degree we are constituted by and controlled by our literacies. At the very least, the portfolio process can aspire to de-institutionalization, within the institution.

But, if portfolios become routine practice each grading period for each student, I pervert the very reasons why I use them: They characterize our unique takes on language, our range of interests, needs, voices, audiences, genres, idiosyncrasies; they demand we wean ourselves from less congruent, more other-driven assessment. But, once portfolios are experienced, we need living time. I worry that too much time and energy is devoted to analyzing our literacy and too little to extending it. Admittedly, portfolios might be designed in countless ways so redundancy is avoidable, and due dates might be staggered so teacher-inundation is unlikely. Still, essentially, what I want students to "get" is that "Aha!" the comes only rarely.

I want students' expressive work to cross media boundaries, to go beyond classroom walls, and to go to work in the world. Language arts students at our university, for example, design projects where they "investigate a present problem and initiate change" as a consequence of their work.

They report their understandings (both process and product) to the class in multimedia presentations. When they ask about including their videos, overheads, skits, surveys, big books, dictionaries, posters, and so on in their final assessment repertoires, I answer with more questions: Who needs this information most? How will you get it to them? By when? What's next?

Last semester, one group who investigated university student health services donated an information video and a custom-made big book for the health services' waiting room. The group who researched "student rip-offs" laminated their posters and hung them in apartment rental offices, parking permit waiting rooms, and Uni-marts. Students who researched campus drinking habits wrote and distributed information sheets and mini-dictionaries to classmates and drinking establishments. The group who studied roommate problems designed such a powerful survey that the university counseling service requested copies for future duplication and distribution.

It's hard to situate videotape, role-play, and music within a portfolio, even one that's sophisticated technologically. If our workshops are to honor multimodal composing, we need to "publish" in alternative modes. Portfolios are notoriously inept at this. I want my students to trust their judgments that they achieved, to move on with their understandings, and to leave me space in my office and my life.

Mihaly Csikszentmihalyi (1990) makes the case for "flow"—that condition of consciousness when "attention can be freely invested to achieve a person's goals. . . . In flow we are more in control of our psychic energy, and everything we do adds order to our consciousness" (p. 40). Clearly, many students experience flow while assembling their portfolios (Graves & Sunstein, 1992; Rief, 1991); but unless the process stimulates significant complexity, flow is unlikely, and the process is little improvement over old rituals. It would be better for these students to seek out literate experiences that produce flow. My favorite question in a writing conference is, What do you really care about here? If the portfolio experience stimulates less caring than, say, revising or initiating writing, or communicating project findings for the class, what purpose does it serve? How necessary is it? What's it for? And because in each class we wrestle as a community and as individuals with assessment, we get better at answering the above questions.

Why was I so enamored with portfolio assessment? I wanted wholes, not parts of persons, in my assessment repertoire. I thought to be whole, one needed to show one's multidimensional writing selves in both breadth and depth. What I did was adopt a new form alongside an old mentality: I nearly basalized the thing by endlessly articulating its possibilities to the extent that one student remarked, "I'd rather have a test."

Now I believe less is more. Because my students and I have experienced what writing assessment looks and feels like through using portfolios, we can conceive of different options to reflect growth.

ACROSS TOWN—MAKING THE NEW CULTURE THEMSELVES

I trust that across town the process for you and your faculty, Jocelyn, will be even better: You are with children daily where you can make possibilities reality. I hope you develop portfolios of your own because, without having experienced that process myself, I doubt I would now act as I do within assessment. I hope you keep portfolio assessment simple and avoid the all-purpose portfolio, pretending to satisfy accountability to everyone. I hope you invite children and families in on decision making from the first day. I hope that within your communities—

> My students and I have experienced what writing assessment looks and feels like through using portfolios.

classroom, home-school, local, and beyond—you articulate literacy values held in common. I hope, as well, you articulate idiosyncratic values. (My fetish for revision need not be yours, nor was it mine when I taught primary grades. My favorite mini-lessons and texts need not be yours, nor were mine the same when I taught elementary students.) Finally, I hope you go slowly and respect Donald Graves' (1992) caution that "we need to explore . . . portfolios for at least another five years" (p. 1). These times are potentially transformative for students, teachers, and parents to be, as Jocelyn put it, "in the driver's seat," since in most school districts, portfolios are still being devised for literacy evaluation. You have the opportunity and responsibility to make portfolios yours. If portfolio development arrives from out-of-town, you and I will have sold out. I hope, in short, that portfolios perform an emancipatory role in literacy evaluation . . . whatever that might mean for our futures as literate individuals within communities.

Now, to get on with teaching writing.

REFERENCES

Bartholomae, D., & Petrosky, A. (1986). *Facts, artifacts and counterfacts.* Upper Montclair, NJ: Boynton/Cook.

Burroway, J. (1987). *Writing Fiction* (2nd ed.). Boston: Little, Brown.

Calkins, L., & Harwayne, S. (1991). *Living between the lines.* Portsmouth, NH: Heinemann.

Csikszentmihalyi, M. (1990). *Flow: The psychology of optimal experience.* New York: Harper & Row.

Flagg, F. (1987). *Fried green tomatoes at the Whistle Stop Cafe.* New York: McGraw-Hill.

Fox, M. (1993). *Radical reflections: Passionate opinions on teaching, learning, and living.* New York: Harcourt Brace.

Gee, J. (1987). What is literacy? *Teaching and Learning, 2,* 3–11.

Graves, D. (1992). Portfolios: Keep a good idea growing. In D. Graves & B. Sunstein (Eds.), *Portfolio portraits* (pp. 1–12). Portsmouth, NH: Heinemann.

Graves, D., & Sunstein, B. (Eds.). (1992). *Portfolio portraits.* Portsmouth, NH: Heinemann.

Mayher, J. (1990). *Uncommon sense.* Portsmouth, NH: Heinemann.

Meyrowitz, J. (1985). *No sense of place.* New York: Oxford University Press.

Murray, D. (1991). *The craft of revision.* Philadelphia, PA: Holt, Rinehart and Winston.

Pappas, C., Kiefer, B., & Levstik, L. (Eds.). (1990). *An integrated language perspective in the elementary school.* White Plains, NY: Longman.

Rief, C. (1991). *Seeking diversity: Language arts with adolescents.* Portsmouth, NH: Heinemann.

Romano, T. (1992). Multigenre research: One college senior. In D. Graves & B. Sunstein (Eds.), *Portfolio portraits* (pp. 146–157). Portsmouth, NH: Heinemann.

Rose, M. (1989). *Lives on the boundary.* New York: Free Press/Macmillan.

Shannon, P. (1994). The social life of basals. In P. Shannon & K. Goodman (Eds.), *Basal readers: A second look* (pp. 201–16). Katonah, NY: Richard C. Owen.

Shaughnessy, M. (1977). *Errors and expectations.* New York: Oxford University Press.

Tierney, R., Carter, M., & Desai, L. (Eds.). (1991). *Portfolio assessments in the reading-writing classroom.* Norwood, MA: Christopher-Gordon.

Wilde, J. (1993). *A door opens: Writing in fifth grade.* Portsmouth, NH: Heinemann.

User-Friendly Portfolios: The Search Goes On

by Susan Mandel Glazer, Katrin-Kaja Rooman, and Kristine Luberto

We have been hearing about "portfolios" for several years now. Many of us are experimenting with them in our classrooms. Some of us are actually utilizing them in effective, efficient ways. What all of us have found is that establishing a portfolio component as part of a learning environment is not easy to do.

> Establishing a portfolio component as part of a learning environment is not easy to do.

In our New Jersey school district, we've experimented with portfolios for approximately two years. Last year, our school began using "literacy portfolios" as tools for assessment. This decision to use them resulted from formal meetings among faculty, reading specialists and school/district administrators, and many informal, chance meetings in the hallways.

TOP OF THE AGENDA

When we began planning for portfolios, we knew that establishing our purposes for using them would be at the top of our agenda. We were finally able to agree that our purposes were:

  • to gather concrete information that demonstrated each student's academic development over time
  • to enable the teacher to assess each student effectively, using a set of benchmarks geared to the individual needs of each child

From *Teaching K–8*, November/December 1994, pp. 105–6. © 1994 by Teaching K–8, Norwalk, CT 06854. Reprinted with permission.

• to enable each child to be involved with self-assessment and developing metacognitive abilities

• to include a component establishing each student's individuality, e.g., attitudinal survey or a piece of information indicating their strengths and/or interests

• to give parents an opportunity to view their child's academic portfolio in an effective and organized format

FLEXIBLE TOOLS

With these purposes in mind, we began to consider what should be included in the portfolios. We knew we wanted some standard measures of development represented, but we also wanted the flexibility to include additional pieces chosen by the teacher and/or student.

> A major concern was the amount of time and effort required to implement the use of portfolios in the daily classroom routines.

Our district does not use standardized tests below third grade. However, we wanted some means of measuring student development in all grades.

A group of teacher volunteers, headed by our vice principal, researched the use of portfolios in other districts, attended workshops, and read "volumes" of information. The group came to the conclusion that we needed to experiment with portfolios that would work best for *our* school.

Our pilot year became one of trial and error and endless questions. Many teachers were concerned about which tests to use to assess comprehension.

We attempted to establish benchmarks for each grade. What would be considered "meaningful" evaluation across grade levels was our concern.

MAJOR CONCERN

We asked questions and analyzed the types of assessment we might use. A major concern was the amount of time and effort required to implement the use of portfolios in the daily classroom routines. There was so much to consider that at times it seemed like an overwhelming task.

At this point, we are continuing to work on developing appropriate benchmarks within and across grade levels for literary tasks. In first grade, for example, extensive modeling is done prior to the activity that serves as a "mark" toward growth.

Two texts we found particularly helpful as resources were *Portfolios and Beyond* by Susan Mandel Glazer and Carol Brown (Christopher-Gordon Publications, 1993) and *Teaching Kids to Spell* by J. Richard Gentry and Jean W. Gillet (Heinemann, 1992).

Glazer and Brown give many useful suggestions concerning collaborative assessment in classrooms. Using Gentry and Gillet's lists of recommended spelling words and activities for both evaluation and instruction gave teachers and students a way to look at spelling progress.

PRIMARY FOCUS

Through it all, we kept our primary focus in the forefront: Portfolios had to be extended beyond a collection of student work.

We believed that portfolios were an *everyday* working tool for both students and teacher and that the teacher's ". . . role in the 'save-the-stuff' process is to support children's choices and guide them to justify selections" (Susan Mandel Glazer, *Teaching K–8*, May 1994).

When students are presented with choices and are involved with self-evaluation, they become responsible for their own learning.

Choices for students' inclusions in the portfolios start in the earliest grades. Eventually, the portfolios will become an integral part of the assessment process. At this point, however, we are still in an early experimental stage with this area of portfolios.

FUTURE LEARNING

Portfolios help students make self-discoveries. They give concrete evidence of what students have learned and a direction for future learning. We have also found that students' metacognitive skills are sharpened when they begin to see learning patterns for what works and what doesn't.

We concentrated our efforts this past year—the second year of our project—on making the portfolios "user-friendly" for both teachers and students. That way, the portfolios could become everyday classroom tools.

EIGHT IDEAS

From our experiences, we developed a list of ideas for teachers who are thinking about using portfolios in their own classrooms. They are as follows:

1. Choose a convenient central location for the portfolios.

2. Select containers that work best for you. (Some of our teachers use shoeboxes.)

3. Model portfolio instructions.

4. Schedule regular conferences with each student. When conferencing, have students spread out all materials so that they can see their progress.

5. Require each student to justify in writing the choices he or she has made. (We found that using a Post-it note was a quick and effective way of doing this.)

6. Use Post-it notes for teacher observations and insights into the individual student.

7. Create a "Proud Portfolio" bulletin board. (We used yarn grids for each student's space. The students enjoyed displaying for others the work of which they were proud.)

8. Help students make the final selection of work at the end of the school year.

CRITIQUING THEIR PEERS

One additional benefit we found from the process was that students, by looking critically at their own work, became better at critiquing the work of their peers in a positive, constructive manner.

We knew we were on the right track when a student in Kristine's second grade class asked to save a dilapidated scrap of paper concerning a rough draft for a biographical piece.

Kristine asked her to justify her request. The student explained that the scrap of paper was the first piece she had ever written that was biographical; thus, it was important to her. In fact, it became a prized entry in her portfolio.

We look back on our year of "trial and error" with mixed feelings. The task of establishing effective and efficient portfolios is difficult, time-consuming, and at times frustrating.

All in all, however, we learned a great deal about our commitment, which is to bring about authentic assessment.

THE RIGHT PATH

We feel we are on the right path. We realize that we have more questions now than when we began the process. As our experience grows, some of our questions will be answered and still others will be raised.

We will continue the use of portfolios in our classrooms this school year, and we will try to make the portfolios as "user-friendly" as we possibly can.

Most of all, through daily use of portfolios, we hope to create in our students an awareness that *they* must be the instigators and assessors of their own intellectual growth and development.

What Makes a Portfolio a Portfolio?

by F. Leon Paulson, Pearl R. Paulson, and Carol A. Meyer

I used all my writing skill to make this paper persuade. Word choice was very important to me." Tony attached these words to a paper in his writing portfolio to explain why the paper was significant to him. His self-reflective statements help illustrate a key value associated with student portfolios and a rationale for using them: portfolios permit instruction and assessment to be woven together in a way that more traditional approaches do not.

This article explores the question, "What makes a portfolio a portfolio?" Let's begin with a definition that we helped formulate while working with a group of educators from seven states under the auspices of the Northwest Evaluation Association[1]:

> Portfolios permit instruction and assessment to be woven together in a way that more traditional approaches do not.

> A portfolio is a purposeful collection of student work that exhibits the student's efforts, progress, and achievements in one or more areas. The collection must include student participation in selecting contents, the criteria for selection, the criteria for judging merit, and evidence of student self-reflection.

The writing portfolios used in Tony's class are in many ways similar to the portfolios artists assemble in order to gain

From *Educational Leadership*, vol. 48, no. 5, February 1991, pp. 60–63. © 1991 by the Association for Supervision and Curriculum Development. Reprinted with permission.

entrance into an art school or to secure a commission. For example, the Pacific Northwest College of Art[2] gives the following rationale for portfolios:

> An application portfolio is a visual representation of who you are as an artist, your history as well as what you are currently doing. . . . It is representing you when you're not present. . . . Part of the evaluation of a portfolio is based on the personal choices [you] make when picking pieces for the portfolio. It tells the school something about [your] current values; that's why you will rarely get a school to be very specific about what they look for in a portfolio. [You] should not be afraid to make choices.

THE PORTFOLIO: A POWERFUL CONCEPT

Portfolios have the potential to reveal a lot about their creators. They can become a window into the students' heads, a means for both staff and students to understand the educational process at the level of the individual learner. They can be powerful educational tools for encouraging students to take charge of their own learning.

Portfolios allow students to assume ownership in ways that few other instructional approaches allow. Portfolio assessment requires students to collect and reflect on examples of their work, providing both an instructional component to the curriculum and offering the opportunity for authentic assessments. If carefully assembled, portfolios become an intersection of instruction and assessment: they are not just instruction or just assessment but, rather, both. Together, instruction and assessment give more than either gives separately.

GUIDELINES FOR REALIZING THAT POWER

Fulfilling the potential of portfolios as an intersection of instruction and assessment is neither simple nor straightforward. We must find new ways for the two processes to work together. Doing so involves answering a question that has no simple answer: "What makes a portfolio a portfolio?" The portfolio is a concept that can be realized in many ways. Portfolios are as varied as the children who create them and as the classrooms in which they are found. However, to preserve those aspects of the portfolio that give the concept its power, we offer this list of guidelines[3]:

1. Developing a portfolio offers the student an opportunity to learn about learning. Therefore, the end product must contain information that shows that a student has engaged in self-reflection.

2. The portfolio is something that is done *by* the student, not *to* the student. Portfolio assessment offers a concrete way for students to learn to value their own work and, by extension, to value themselves as learners. Therefore, the student must be involved in selecting the pieces to be included.

> **The portfolio is something that is done *by* the student, not *to* the student.**

3. The portfolio is separate and different from the student's cumulative folder. Scores and other cumulative folder information that are held in central depositories should be included in a portfolio only if they take on new meaning within the context of the other exhibits found there.

4. The portfolio must convey explicitly or implicitly the student's activities; for example, the rationale (purpose for forming the portfolio), intents (its goals), contents (the actual displays), standards (what is good and not-so-good performance), and judgments (what the contents tell us).[4]

5. The portfolio may serve a different purpose during the year from the purpose it serves at the end. Some material may be kept because it is instructional, for example, partially finished work on problem areas. At the end of the year, however, the portfolio may contain only material that the student is willing to make public.

6. A portfolio may have multiple purposes, but these must not conflict. A student's personal goals and interests are reflected in his or her selection of materials, but information included may also reflect the interests of teachers, parents, or the district. One purpose that is almost universal in student portfolios is showing progress on the goals represented in the instructional program.

7. The portfolio should contain information that illustrates growth. There are many ways to demonstrate growth. The most obvious is by including a series of examples of actual school performance that show how the student's skills have improved. Changes observed on interest inventories, records of

outside activities such as reading, or on attitude measures are other ways to illustrate a student's growth.

8. Finally, many of the skills and techniques that are involved in producing effective portfolios do not happen by themselves. By way of support, students need models of portfolios, as well as examples of how others develop and reflect upon portfolios.

There are a considerable variety of portfolio assessment projects appearing in schools, reflecting the fact that portfolio assessment is a healthy and robust concept. We recommend, however, that when designing programs or purchasing commercial portfolio assessment materials, educators reflect on the eight aspects of the portfolio that we believe give the concept its power. We offer our list as a way of initiating thoughtful critiques.

A BROAD LOOK AT LEARNING

Portfolios offer a way of assessing student learning that is quite different from traditional methods. While achievement tests offer outcomes in units that can be counted and accounted, portfolio assessment offers the opportunity to observe students in a broader context: taking risks, developing creative solutions, and learning to make judgments about their own performances.

A portfolio, then, is a portfolio when it provides a complex and comprehensive view of student performance in context. It is a portfolio when the student is a participant in, rather than the object of, assessment. Above all, a portfolio is a portfolio when it provides a forum that encourages students to develop the abilities needed to become independent, self-directed learners.

NOTES

1. This working definition grew out of discussions at a conference on "Aggregating Portfolio Data" held at Union, Washington, in August 1990. For more information, see: *White Paper on Aggregating Portfolio Data,* rev. ed., (1990), by C. Meyer and S. Schuman, which is available from the Northwest Evaluation Association, 5 Centerpointe Dr., Lake Oswego, OR 97035.

2. Pacific Northwest College of Art, (1985), *Preparing your Application Portfolio* (pamphlet); available from the college at 1219 S.W. Park, Portland OR 97205.

3. This list draws on discussions on metacognition (thinking about thinking) held at conferences on portfolio assessment in December 1989 and August 1990. Participants were from seven states and included teachers, curriculum and assessment specialists, administrators, and representatives of state departments of education. We would like to acknowledge the contributions of the 57 people who participated.

4. See F. L. Paulson and P. R. Paulson, "How Do Portfolios Measure Up? A Cognitive Model for Assessing Portfolios," paper presented at the conference of the Northwest Evaluation Association on "Aggregating Portfolio Data," Union, Washington, August 1990.

The Portfolio Connection: Real-World Examples

by Robin Fogarty, Kay Burke, and Susan Belgrad

The object of education is to prepare the young to educate themselves throughout their lives.—Robert Maynard Hutchins

T he quest for more authentic assessments to complement the more traditional measures of evaluation is manifested in the concept of learner portfolios. While the portfolio it-self focuses on the *products* of the learner's efforts, in current practice the emphasis is also on the *process* of portfolio development (Wolf 1989).

In fact, it is the process, in its simplest form, that becomes the focus. This process encompasses three macrophases: collection, selection, and reflection (Hamm & Adams, 1991). For the teacher who is beginning the adventure with portfolio assessment, these three stages are the basic steps needed for portfolio development. As the process becomes more clearly defined, however, a number of secondary phases come into play.

The complete list of options for portfolio development include ten considerations (see Figure 1).

In this discussion, each phase of the process opens with a real-world example and ends with a list of ideas for immediate use. While some of the scenarios present examples of portfolio development in the *classroom,* others illustrate similar uses in the *staff room.* However, whether used with the student learners or as a professional development tool, "the portfolio connection" is an important intersection between instruction and assessment in today's schools (Paulson, Paulson, & Meyer 1991).

From *Best Practices for the Learner-Centered Classroom: A Collection of Articles,* pp. 303–14. © 1995 by IRI/Skylight Training and Publishing, Inc.

Figure 1
Portfolio Development Options

1. PROJECT purposes and uses
2. COLLECT and organize
3. SELECT valued artifacts
4. INTERJECT personality
5. REFLECT metacognitively
6. INSPECT and self-assess goals
7. PERFECT, evaluate, and grade (if you must)
8. CONNECT and conference
9. INJECT AND EJECT to update
10. RESPECT accomplishments and show with pride

PROJECT PURPOSES AND USES

In Whitby, Ontario, an instructional facilitator for the Durham Board of Education immerses teachers in portfolio use by having them keep portfolios of their own. They gather items from their teaching over a predetermined period of time and meet periodically for discussion. By experiencing the process, teachers are able to "walk the talk" about the essential elements of portfolios as assessment tools. As a result, they are better able to share their expertise with both the students and the parents.

To ensure effective use of the portfolio, it is critical that teachers look at the "big picture" to determine the many uses of portfolios. They need to ask hard questions: Why involve the students in the ongoing process of gathering artifacts? How are the portfolios going to be used? What is the real purpose? What are the potential uses, overuses, and abuses of portfolios for assessment purposes and beyond?

The purposes of portfolios tend to fall into three distinct categories: personal, academic, and professional (Burke, Fogarty, & Belgrad, 1994). Of course, within each of these broad categories, a range of models exist (see Figure 2).

Figure 2
Portfolio Models

Personal	Academic	Professional
Hobbies	Graded	College Admission
Collections	Integrated	Employability
Scrapbooks	Cooperative	Performance Review
Journals	Multi-year	

COLLECT AND ORGANIZE

At a conference in Battle Creek, Michigan, one teacher shared how her primary students are proud of the personally tailored, family-size cereal box portfolios they bring into the classroom, decorate, and use to store artifacts of their work. Easily obtained, just the right size, handy, and accessible for the students, these cereal box portfolios are marvelously versatile starter kits. Both the children and the teacher regularly add items to the portfolio, which are akin to student mailboxes. Periodically, artifacts are sorted and weeded out as the boxes become too full.

Students start the ongoing process of gathering and collecting their work for possible inclusion in their final portfolios. Deciding how to put things together for easy reference and logical continuity requires a number of considerations, including the *type of container* (notebook, box, envelope, file folder, or photo album); the *labeling technique* (tabs, table of contents, or registry); the *order of things* (sequential, prioritized, thematic, or random); and, of course, the *overall look* of the collection (academic, aesthetic, personal, or eclectic). Order reigns over chaos when the number and assortment of things can easily be managed using these ideas (see Figure 3).

SELECT VALUED ARTIFACTS

Jane Franklin, an instructional facilitator for the Durham Board of Education in Ontario, leads a study group comprised of primary teachers who are interested in learning about portfolios. To help them understand the selection process, as applied to portfolio

---

Figure 3
Portfolio Organization Options

Storage	Flow	Tools
Hanging file	Collecting	Tabs
Colored folder	Selecting	Colored dots
Accordion folder	Reflecting	Table of contents
Cereal boxes	Perfecting	Registry
Computer disks	Connecting	Labels
Notebooks		Index

---

management, she uses the "bookshelf" activity. Each teacher is asked to select a representational sampling of books from her personal collection to share with the group. Interestingly, as the teachers mull over their selections, they invariably begin to selectively abandon some of their favorites in order to give a true representation. Teachers simulate this activity with students, asking them to select from their collections of shells, stamps, or coins as they prepare for portfolio selection.

Selection is to abandonment as *collection* is to abundance. Decisions must be made about the context and contents of the portfolio based on the intent and purposes that the portfolio serves. Alignment to the goals and standards must be considered. Periodically, candidate artifacts must face the selection process. Decisions must be made and the final vote taken as nominated items are included and excluded.

General guidelines may state the number of items, the type, stages and phases, variety, and/or personal choices. Key words that guide that selection process are "Who?" "When?" and "What?" (see Figure 4).

INTERJECT PERSONALITY

In the Richmond Schools in British Columbia, an art teacher requires students to create a portfolio of work for the cartooning class. Throughout the semester, students keep a journal of ideas for cartoon characters. Students also collect finished products and artifacts in an art portfolio (much like designers, architects, illustrators,

---

Figure 4
Guiding Questions for Selection

Who?	When?	What?
Self-select	Parent conference	Representative work
Teacher selects	Quarters	
Student and teacher select	Semesters	Best work
	End of year	Significant work
Peers	Cumulative	Work in progress
Juried		Biography of work

---

photographers, fashion designers, and political cartoonists keep).
Students in the cartooning class review and preview their work over
time and interject their personal touches to the collection for the se-
mester end submittal.

Each portfolio is as unique as one's fingerprint. No two look exactly alike, even if they contain similar elements, because the student tailors the look of the portfolio to reflect an up-close-and-personal view that allows a more intimate look at the total person.

Some say that the portfolio is, in fact, a window into the personality, skills, and talents of its owner. Typically, one interjects personality and pizazz into the portfolio through several critical elements, including the cover, the organizational scheme, the page layout, and the mood or tone reflected in the content and design (see Figure 5).

Figure 5
Interjecting Personality into Portfolios

Cover	Organization	Page Layout	Mood/Tone
Color	Shape	Straight	Humorous
Design	Size	Geometric	Serious
Texture	Type	Cluster	Aesthetic
Style	File or pile	Threads	Technical

Figure 6
Stages of Metacognitive Reflection

Planning	Monitoring	Evaluating
Imagery	Labeling	Registering
Strategic plan	Self-questioning	Anecdotal stories

REFLECT METACOGNITIVELY

As part of the district's partnership project, one teacher took a three-day visit to schools in Vermont. She returned to her school in Pickering, Ontario, with a wealth of knowledge, information, and practical strategies for implementing portfolios in her math classes. In fact, she put together a handbook to guide the development of the portfolios and to promote genuine understanding of math concepts and problem-solving models for her grade nine "transition years" students. Throughout the portfolio development, students are frequently required to comment on their metacognitive thinking by responding to thought-provoking statements about their best work and how math portfolios might be improved (Bowers, 1994).

The true essence of the student portfolio is revealed as the students highlight the subtleties of the selected work. Each piece needs several metacognitive moments, moments when the student surveys her portfolio plan, monitors and adjusts her collection to date, and evaluates the value of each artifact, both as an individual piece and in the grand scheme of things. One relatively easy way to do this is to label each piece and provide the needed rationale. These labels provide the running monologue that brings the portfolio to life at various stages of metacognitive reflection (see Figure 6).

INSPECT AND SELF-ASSESS GOALS

On Chicago's West Side, a neighborhood school (K–8) has embraced the visual and performing arts as its focus for integrating the curricula. One innovative technique teachers employ is videotaped assessment. Each student is given a videotape that is donated by a local firm. Each student is taped participating in significant

---

Figure 7
Portfolio Inspection Steps

Getting Started	Goal Setting	Final Decisions
Use stem statements	Logs	Standards
Build checklist	Journals	Criteria
Set criteria	Learning lists	Rubric
Develop scoring rubrics	Double-entry journal	Best work
Give feedback	Reflective journal	Significant work
Review standards		Representative work

---

schoolwide and classroom events. The tape travels back and forth to the home and school as the student shares highlights of her school day with her family.

The student inspects her entire collection of work for insights. This time is designated for the student to review both long-term and short-term goals and to note strengths and weaknesses.

This stage is aptly labeled "inspect" because the student self-evaluates her overall direction and focus. It's the moment of truth that signals the learner whether or not she is on track and what measures might be needed to align with her aims and goals. There seem to be three distinct steps that help students to inspect: getting started, goal setting, and final decisions (see Figure 7).

PERFECT, EVALUATE, AND GRADE (IF YOU MUST)

A portfolio scoring rubric solves the ever-present problem of grading in a sixth grade class at a school in upstate New York. Using the rubric as a guide to evaluate the entire portfolio, students are clear on the criteria and indicators needed to obtain the grade they want (1=Not ready, 2=Acceptable, 3=Out of sight). Interestingly, the rubric is scored separately by both the teacher and the students. The students may improve each item and resubmit them for the final grade.

Figure 8
Portfolio Grading Options

Each Artifact	Selected	Entire Portfolio	Weighted Scores
Previously graded	Student selects	Rubric scoring	Predetermined
Item by item	Teacher selects	Holistic grade	Student decides
	Randomly chosen	Averaged grade	Teacher decides

In preparation for the portfolio conference with parents, students perfect their portfolios by adding finishing touches. At this stage, both the teacher and the student take a final look.

Students examine the entire portfolio with a special eye for inconsistencies, such as missing labels or torn or tattered artifacts, as well as for accuracy in the registry.

Teachers, on the other hand, often use this stage to evaluate the portfolio formally. They apply scoring rubrics and assign grades (or a grade) to the portfolio. In fact, the options for grading are surprisingly varied (see Figure 8).

CONNECT AND CONFERENCE

Students in a seventh grade class in Richmond, British Columbia, use their portfolios to help them prepare for three-way, student-led parent conferences. First, they survey the myriad artifacts in their collections to aid in their sketches of Venn diagrams that show how the subject-related items integrate with one another (see Figure 9). Then, using the portfolio itself and their Venn diagrams as notes, they actually lead the parent/teacher/student conference and share reflections of their work.

Student portfolios are assembled, arranged, rearranged, and refined in preparation for the portfolio conference. This is a crucial step in portfolio use as an assessment tool because, as students know, what is inspected is respected. If portfolios are to be valued as viable complements to more traditional assessments, they must be critiqued by others. The conference format offers a number of options (see Figure 10).

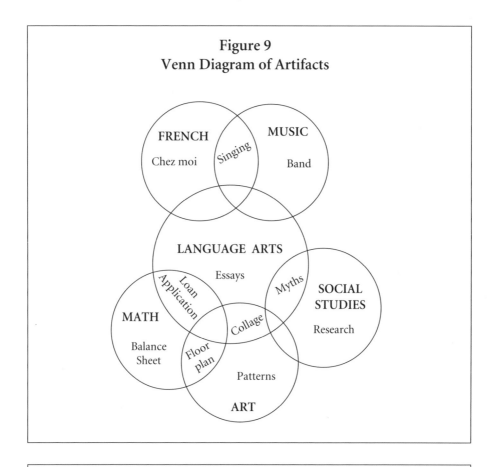

Figure 9
Venn Diagram of Artifacts

Figure 10
Portfolio Conference Options

Traditional	**Student Conducted**	**Three-Way**	**Home**
Teacher-led	Student prepares	Student/	Student/
Teacher and	Student presents	parent/	parent
parent present		teacher	

INJECT AND EJECT TO UPDATE

A manager at the southern consortium in San Diego, California, uses the Professional Development Portfolio to evaluate the impact of staff development services and to assist planning teams in making strategic decisions. The Teacher's Briefcase, developed by Mary

---

Figure 11
Inject/Eject Options

Periodic	**Momentary**	**Shift in Focus**	**Spontaneous**
Routine	Make-over	Radical	Refresher
Predetermined	Purposeful	Change in	Spring cleaning
Intervals	Quick	direction	Unplanned
		Different effect	

Dietz, consists of three separate items: a journal with structured entry activities; a mini-guide that describes what to do; and a canvas bag to hold videotapes, student artifacts, and the journal. A critical element that gives teachers insight into managing portfolios is the artifact registry. This is a running record of artifacts logged in and logged out of the portfolio in order to keep the sheer number of items somewhat manageable. It also provides an at-a-glance inventory of items, which is a keen management technique (Dietz, 1991).

While the focus of the portfolio is often the parent conference, ideally the portfolio process extends beyond that immediate use and becomes a true collection of work over time that the student continues throughout her school career and beyond. People who use portfolios as part of the college entrance and career interview processes take great pains to continually inject and eject artifacts to update their portfolio and to reflect not only past, but also current work. There are several options for updating the portfolio (see Figure 11).

RESPECT ACCOMPLISHMENTS AND SHOW WITH PRIDE

Teachers in a field-based master's program in Wheeling, Illinois, use portfolio exhibitions to display "biographies of work" (Wolf, 1989) that depict the processes and products of their action research project. A site facilitator orchestrates the exhibition in the spring prior to the graduation ceremonies. The exhibition serves as a culminating activity in which teachers in the two-year program share their work with other professionals. First-year students in the program are invited to view the exhibits to prepare for their next year's work on their own master's projects.

Figure 12
Elements in a Portfolio Exhibition

Goal	Audience	Time/Type	Media Options
Summative	Parents	Browsing	Video
Formative	Peers	Presenting	Audio
Admission	Public	Responding	Computer disk
Employment	Mentors	Traveling	Slides
Commission	Apprentices	Group/ individual	Multimedia

The primary purpose for portfolios in schools today is to enhance the assessment process. The actual artifacts of work are evidence of student development beyond the test score or arbitrary grade point average. Myriad uses for portfolios are beginning to surface, however, as their actual use becomes more prevalent. In fact, the student may find a portfolio exhibition to be a viable tool to use in certain circumstances.

The exhibition brings the work alive. As the student represents her pieces to others, the viewers gain valuable insight into the person behind the work. There are many points to consider in presenting one's portfolio at an exhibition (see Figure 12).

In the words of George Bernard Shaw, "What we want is to see the child in pursuit of knowledge, not knowledge in pursuit of the child." The portfolio connection and these real-world examples illustrate that very concept.

REFERENCES

Belanoff, P., & Dickson, M. (1991). *Portfolios: Process and product.* Portsmouth, NH: Boyton & Cook Publishers.

Burke, K. (1994). *The mindful school: How to assess authentic learning.* Palatine, IL: IRI/Skylight Publishing.

Burke, K. (1992). *Authentic assessment: A collection.* Palatine, IL: IRI/Skylight Publishing.

Burke, K., Fogarty, R., & Belgrad, S. (1994). *The mindful school: The portfolio connection.* Palatine, IL: IRI/Skylight Publishing.

Costa, A., Bellanca, J., & Fogarty, R. (1992). *If minds matter: A foreword to the future, Vol. 2.* Palatine, IL: IRI/Skylight Publishing.

Dietz, M. E. (1991). *Professional development portfolio: Facilitator's guide and journal.* San Ramon, CA: Frameworks.

Gardner, H. (1993). *Multiple intelligences: The theory in practice.* New York: Basic Books.

Hamm, M., & Adams, D. (1991, May). Portfolio: It's not just for artists anymore. *The Science Teacher,* pp. 18–21.

Hansen, J. (1992, May). Literacy portfolios: Helping students know themselves. *Educational Leadership,* pp. 66–68.

Kallick, B. (1992). Evaluation: A collaborative process. In A. L. Costa, J. A. Bellanca, & R. Fogarty (Eds.), *If minds matter: A foreword to the future, Vol. 2* (pp. 313–19). Palatine, IL: IRI/Skylight Publishing.

Stiggins, R. J. (1991, March). Assessment literacy. *Phi Delta Kappan,* pp. 534–539.

Paulson, F. L., Paulson, P. R., & Meyer, C. A. (1991, February). What makes a portfolio a portfolio? *Educational Leadership,* pp. 60–63.

Stiggins, R. J. (1985, October). Improving assessment where it means the most: In the classroom. *Educational Leadership,* pp. 69–74.

Wiggins, G. (1990, August). Put portfolios to the test. *Instructor,* p. 51.

Wolf, D. P. (1989, April). Portfolio assessment: Sampling student work. *Educational Leadership,* pp. 35–39.

Portfolio Assessment: Sampling Student Work

by Dennie Palmer Wolf

For the last two years, a consortium of administrators, teachers, and researchers in the Pittsburgh schools has been searching for alternatives to standardized assessment. In that work we have found that the world brims over with examples of the differences between testing as we know it in schools and the reflective self-evaluation that is inseparable from pursuing virtually any kind of worthwhile work.

Some examples? Last summer when the Dodgers were heating up, I heard a radio announcer tease pitcher Orel Hershiser about keeping a journal. Hershiser wasn't fazed. He simply said human memory is too faulty and he cares too much about what makes him crackerjack one day and just average the next not to keep track. Several days later, I visited a small gallery where they show artists' books and working drawings. Inside, the walls and cases were crammed with sketches by Ree Morton, a sculptor who began studying art in her thirties, surrounded by young children, drafting and writing on top of the washing machine. There on the gallery walls was evidence of another kind of evaluation: Morton would stalk an idea from inception to final work, making version after version after version. Then, two days ago, I listened to Sonny Rollins reminiscing on a jazz show. He was remembering how, smack in the middle of gigs and tours, he decided to "step out to find a new sound." He left the world of clubs and concert halls to practice hours at a time

From *Educational Leadership*, vol. 46, no. 7, April 1989, pp. 35–39. © 1989 by the Association for Supervision and Curriculum Development. Reprinted with permission.

where the acoustics would let him get inside the music—solo on the bridges of New York City.

Here is both promise and trouble. The promise lies in the demonstration of how demanding and thoughtful we can be about shaping work that matters to us. The trouble lies in recognizing how we ignore this capacity in schools. Never do we stop to ask how we could make our evaluative gatekeeping model the kind of self-observation and informed critique that separates ball tossers from fine pitchers, doodlers from artists, or instrumentalists from musicians. Yet virtually every student walks out of school into years of long-term projects: raising children, building a house, running a farm, writing a novel, or becoming a better lab technician. All of these projects require moment-to-moment monitoring, Monday morning quarterbacking, and countless judgments of errors and worth. Unfortunately, very little in the way we now structure assessment in schools names or encourages those lifelong skills.

> Much school-based assessment actually *prevents* students from becoming thoughtful respondents to, and judges of, their own work.

Even in a time when increasing numbers of educators are working to diversify and humanize the way we evaluate student learning, much school-based assessment actually *prevents* students from becoming thoughtful respondents to, and judges of, their own work. The "surprise" nature of many test items, the emphasis on objective knowledge, the once-over and one-time nature of most exams—all offer students lessons that are destructive to their capacity to thoughtfully judge their own work: (1) assessment comes from without, it is not a personal responsibility; (2) what matters is not the full range of your intuitions and knowledge but your performance on the slice of skills that appear on tests; (3) first-draft work is good enough; and (4) achievement matters to the exclusion of development.

ALTERNATIVES FROM THE ARTS AND HUMANITIES

These issues about evaluating student learning have recently been aggravated by debates about what counts as knowledge and learning in the arts and humanities. On the one hand, critics like Bennett, Finn, Hirsch, and Ravitch argue that the first obligation of humanities education is to provide students with a considerable factual knowledge of Western history and culture. On the other hand, a coalition of projects and people argue that students cannot learn and retain facts unless they learn how to *think* about those facts. Therefore, from the earliest age, students must learn the processes characteristic of the humanities: how to question, investigate, think, and write. Certainly another of these processes is self-knowledge and reflection, what the artist Ben Shahn once referred to as the ability to be "the spontaneous imaginer and the inexorable critic all at once." But this capacity may be squeezed out of schooling if current critiques of education lead to a relentless push for coverage of facts.

Among these contending voices are the designers of the new Civilizations of the Americas course at Stanford University, the College Board's EQuality project, and the CHART (Collaborative for Humanities and Art) programs funded by the Rockefeller Foundation and designed to bring both critical and creative thinking to students normally disbarred from anything but functional education.

Included among the Rockefeller projects is PROPEL, the three-way consortium mentioned earlier. PROPEL brings together the Pittsburgh Public Schools, Educational Testing Service, and Project Zero at the Harvard Graduate School of Education in an effort to demonstrate that it is possible to assess the thinking processes characteristic of the arts and humanities in rigorous, but undistorted, ways. Central to this work are two aims. The first is to design ways of evaluating student learning that, while providing information to teachers and school systems, will also model personal responsibility in questioning and reflecting on one's own work. The second is to find ways of capturing growth over time so that students can become informed and thoughtful assessors of their own histories as learners.

To accomplish these aims, the teachers and researchers in PROPEL have asked experts—artists, musicians, and writers—how they sample and judge their own life work. Time and again, something like Orel Hershiser's diary, Ree Morton's stack of sketchbooks, or Rollins' sustained practicing surfaces. Whatever the medium, the message is the same: thinkers and inventors often keep longitudinal collections of their ideas, drafts, and questions. They use these as a kind of storehouse of possibilities for later work, valuing them as a record of where they have been and reading them for a sharp sense of their own signatures and uncertainties. Building on these examples, PROPEL teachers and researchers have developed systems of portfolio assessment in the visual arts, music, and writing.

> **Thinkers and inventors often keep longitudinal collections of their ideas, drafts, and questions.**

PORTFOLIOS

PROPEL portfolios have developed some distinguishing characteristics. To begin, students collect more than a diverse body of finished work. In fact, they gather what we have come to call *biographies of works*, a *range of works*, and *reflections*. A biography of a work reveals the geology of different moments that underlies the production of any major project. Among young musicians preparing for a concert, such a biography includes regular tape recordings of a particularly telling section of a piece. For a young writer it might include the notes, diagrams, drafts, and final version of a poem.

The range of works is deliberately diverse. A student artist might include collages, prints, photos or portraits, landscapes, and still lifes. The young writer might bring together pieces as diverse as journal entries, letters, poems, or essays from social studies classes.

Reflections are documents (or even audiotapes) that come from moments when teachers ask students to return to their collections of work, taking up the stance of an informed critic or autobiographer, noticing what is characteristic, what has changed with time, or what still remains to be done. At the end of any given semester or year, teachers offer students a still longer period of time to study their collections, selecting several works that best exemplify what has changed for the student in that time. These works, along with student and teacher commentaries, become a final portfolio that can be passed along as a continuing document from year to year.

WHY BOTHER?

Portfolios are messy. They demand intimate and often frighteningly subjective talk with students. Portfolios are work. Teachers who ask students to read their own progress in the "footprints" of their works have to coax and bicker with individuals who are used to being assessed. Halfway through the semester, at least a half dozen recalcitrants will lose every paper or sketch or tape they have ever owned. More important, teachers have to struggle to read and make sense of whole works and patterns of growth. Hence, hard questions arise: "Why bother? What comes out of portfolio-based assessment?" The immediate answer lies in integrity and the validity of the information we gain about how and what students learn. But that's far from all.

> Portfolios are messy. They demand intimate and often frighteningly subjective talk with students.

Student Responsibility

In the fall of last year, Kathy Howard faced an ordinary class of 8th graders who had not written more than the answers to chapter questions and who had certainly never been asked to reflect on their progress as writers. In the ensuing months she began to insist that they write essays, journals, and poems. At intervals of several months, she asked her students to select two pieces: one that didn't satisfy them and another that they liked. Her students studied these pieces and wrote down what they noticed about themselves as writers. Sometimes she left students on their own; at other times she discussed the various dimensions of their writing that they might consider. As students continued to write, they revisited their earlier choices, seeing whether old favorites held up in the light of their own evolving standards. After eight months, the climate around writing had changed dramatically; part of writing was now the responsibility to know where you were and what you thought. By early June, the classroom dialogue had acquired a sound that was tough yet meditative:

"I want you to look at what you chose last time as your most satisfying piece and your least satisfying piece. You don't have to change them, but I want to give you the chance to re-evaluate them. Something that once looked good to you may look different now, or you might see something new in a piece you once thought wasn't much.

"Feel free to conference with each other. Go ahead and ask someone else's opinion. But be sure you really give them a chance to read what you have written. Don't just wave a paper in front of their face and ask them."

A student calls: "If we have two satisfying pieces, is that okay?"

"Yes, just be sure you know what you see in each of them."

Kathy pauses beside another student who is shuffling papers. "Rocky, show me what you are using."

"Is this the right one?"

"I don't care which one you choose. I'm just here to listen to your ideas."

He smiles and takes a paper out and holds it up. Kathy reads over his shoulder. "Nice choice. Now why?" Rocky begins to read the paper out loud to her. Kathy jokes: "No, you need to tell me. Think out loud about your writing."

Rocky looks quizzical.

"I want to know why you chose what you did. See, if I chose, I would probably choose different things for *my* reasons."

This slice of life in the classroom illustrates how portfolios can promote a climate of reflection. Words like *think, choose,* and *risk* run throughout the conversation, which is punctuated by pauses for reflection. The answer to a question is not to be found in the text, but in thinking back to earlier times, comparing pieces, and struggling to put your intuitions into words. Kathy hasn't abdicated her role as teacher, but she uses that role to insist that her students go back to their own work, requiring that they construct their own autobiographies as learners. Time and again, she brings the conversation back to what they notice, value, or worry over. She makes her students responsible for taking the lead in evaluating their work.

Enlarging the View of What's Learned

Because portfolios contain a range of work—fiction, poems, essays, journal entries—students come to see what is under development quite differently. While all of them still include neatness and good grammar among the dimensions of change they notice, students also come to see themselves as authors who write differently for different audiences or who make distinctive choices about how they convey information. By way of example, consider what Jeff, an 8th grader, has to say when he reflects on a piece of fiction writing based on Poe's poem "The Raven":

> I had a hard time being the Raven. I knew it right away. So I tried to be really creative, well, sort of crazy. Now I would put some more basic story into it, I would take some of the abstractness out, put some real experiences into it. I wouldn't have left the story so blank.

Later on, when he talks about his essays on books like *Animal Farm,* he relies on a different kind of criteria:

> It's analyzing Napoleon's whole plan for how to get power. I showed each different step and how it came to a conclusion. I didn't use any creative writing. I liked being able to remember about all those things. I could really lay out such a giant story into a page and a half. [I like it when] you can really wrestle with ideas.

A Place for Process

Any writer's work unfolds over time, starting with incubation, changing into notes, undergoing revision, settling into its near-final form, and zigzagging between these different moments as well. In fact, knowing how to pursue the work of writing is as much a part of what is learned as is the sense for where a semicolon goes or how dialogue ought to sound.

At the very simplest level, many of the portfolio pieces are fat stacks of pages that tell the story of the piece's evolution. Such unusual data allow students as well as teachers to form new questions about writing development. Rather than just comparing final pieces, students can investigate how their own revising or editing skills changed over time. Since their pieces don't disappear, students can afford to let ideas incubate and to take enormous trouble over the small changes that distinguish a third draft from a handsomely crafted final work. . . .

A Developmental Point of View

It is no accident that many of the anecdotes offered here take the form of narratives, full of words like *then, before,* and *later.* The use of portfolios engages students in constructing a story—a long-term account—of what and how they learn. As they page through their collections of writing in April or June, they are struck by what they have learned. But that in itself is a story. With time, experience, and conversation, students' ability to read their own portfolios with depth and understanding also develops. Early on, students appraise their own work using only standard and flat-footed criteria: neatness, length, or the grade written at the top. As little as six months later, they notice and care about a widened range of characteristics: how effective a story is, how unusual the words in a poem are, whether the ideas and arguments in an essay are sharp. Moreover, their judgment is variegated; they know a piece can open with fireworks and fizzle in closing. They can point out moments where their writing sails and where it "got away."

What emerges is not just insight about paragraphs or pieces. Talking to students at the end of the school year, one finds that they know their own histories as writers. As one young poet, Justin Brown, remarked:

> When I look back, I see my poems were very basic in the beginning; they were all rhymed haiku because that was all I knew about. Then I experimented with going with the feelings or ideas . . . don't kill yourself going over the rhymes, go with what you feel. I did that for two months. Then I started compacting them, shortening them to make deeper meaning. I could see that it would make more of a point if I washed out the *the's* and *and's* and *if's.* Now I am working on something different—the morals. If one day my mom's car broke down, I might write that night about how a fish got caught, or the feeling of not being able to swim. I am not trying to write how I feel only, but metaphors . . .

> The use of portfolios engages students in constructing a story— a long-term account—of what and how they learn.

TWO FACES

This study has two faces. One is a wholly different way of assessing writing. Within the framework of this project, teachers have begun to talk about using portfolios to widen the range of what they consider development. They don't ignore mechanics and usage, but the talk heats up as they move on to asking one another how they can judge what a student knows about the writing process; how well a student understands the demands of writing journals, poems, and essays; how many risks a young writer is taking.

At the same time, teachers are using these same portfolios to look at their *own* skills and development. At least once a year, a letter arrives in the mail asking teachers to select three to five folders that illustrate exceptional, moderate, or limited progress in writing. The letter alerts teachers that a supervisor will be coming to talk with them about writing. The conference is a time to describe how they are teaching a variety of types of writing, how they encourage students to engage in the several phases of the writing process, and how they comment on and critique student work. Several weeks later, the supervisor and the teacher grab a cup of coffee before school or in a "prep" period and then sit down to "do portfolios." These discussions may be a teacher's chance to talk about what portfolios contribute to student assessment, or the portfolios may serve to highlight places where a particular teacher struggles. But, in either case, during that half hour, teachers take active responsibility for portraying *their* work; they examine many facets of teaching; they don't use tests or first-draft writing samples but evidence of the writing process and the back-and-forth between teacher and student. The result is not a score on a teachers' exam. Instead, it is a reflection on a sample of work. Like student portfolios, it offers a humane, useful, and generative portrait of development—one that a teacher, like a student, can learn from long after the isolated moment of assessment.

> At the same time, teachers are using these same portfolios to look at their *own* skills and development.

Author's note: I would like to acknowledge the close collaboration of students, teachers, and supervisors in the Pittsburgh Public Schools. This work was developed from a paper presented April 8, 1988, at the American Educational Research Association Meeting, New Orleans, Louisiana. The research reported here was supported by a grant from the Division of Arts and Humanities at the Rockefeller Foundation.

Portfolio is the quarterly newsletter of the PROPEL project. It prints writings by teachers and researchers and provides samples of student work and the different forms of assessment being developed. Available from Project Zero at [326 Longfellow Hall, Harvard Graduate School of Education, 13 Appian Way, Cambridge, MA 02138-3752].

RECOMMENDED READINGS

Brandt, R. (December 1987/January 1988). "On Assessment in the Arts: A Conversation with Howard Gardner." *Educational Leadership, 45,* 4: 30–34.

Wolf, D.P. (1986). "All the Pieces That Go into It: The Multiple Stances of Arts Education": In *Aesthetics in Education: The Missing Dimension,* edited by A. Hurwitz. Mattituck, Md.: Amercon Press.

Wolf, D.P. "Artistic Learning: What and Where Is It?" *Journal of Aesthetic Education* 22, 1: 144–55.

Wolf, D.P. (December 1987/January 1988). "Opening Up Assessment." *Educational Leadership* 45, 4: 24–29.

Zessoules, R. (1988). "A Better Balance." In *Beyond DBAE: The Case for Multiple Visions of Art Education,* edited by J. Burton, A. Lederman, and P. London. North Dartmouth, Mass.: Southeastern Massachusetts University.

Electronic Portfolios— Some Pivotal Questions

by Christopher Moersch and Louis M. Fisher III

T he emergence of electronic portfolios on the educational landscape is the result of two major innovations—one pedagogical, the other technological. Education's renewed commitment to concept/process-based learning and its empha-sis on relevancy and authentic applications have created a grow-ing demand for dynamic assessment strat-egies and instruments that measure mul-tiple dimensions of a student's academic progress. Extending beyond a paper-and-pencil format, this new breed of assess-ment strategies embraces a wide variety of media (e.g., pictures, sound, video, computer-based multimedia presenta-tions) to document student success across the curriculum.

> **From the technologi-cal front, recent advances . . . have made electronic portfolios a reality.**

From the technological front, recent advances in micro-processors and mass storage devices, coupled with the prolifera-tion of inexpensive multimedia authoring tools, scanners, digi-tal cameras, personal digital assistants (PDAs), and bar code readers, have made electronic portfolios a reality. Electronic portfolio technology affords us the ability to import/export large quantities of data, attach seemingly endless work samples for immediate access or long-term storage, increase the level of authentic communication between the home and the class-room, and prepare students for the school-to-work transition

From *Learning and Leading with Technology,* vol. 23, no. 2, October 1995, pp. 10–15. © 1995 by the International Society for Technology in Education. Reprinted with permission.

with the aid of career or résumé-based portfolios stored on a re-cordable CD-ROM (CD-R).

Similar to the interest in word processors, the growing interest in electronic portfolios is, in part, due to their linkage with a successful predecessor. Before word processors, we used typewriters faithfully to prepare our written correspondence. A similar case can be made for electronic portfolios. For decades, teachers have used text-based portfolios to collect student work samples even though the primary motive was for short-term storage rather than long-term assessment. Today, the growing fascination with portfolios stems from their role as assessment tools to document student success against a specific set of content and performance standards. Many states, including Kentucky, Oregon, and Vermont, are actively employing student portfolios as a means of assessing student outcomes in specific content areas (e.g., Kentucky-Mathematics) or across the curriculum (e.g., Oregon's Certificate of Initial Mastery and Certificate of Advanced Mastery).

> Such questions as "How can I minimize storage requirements?" dominate any discussion about electronic portfolios.

Though advances in technology have paved the way for electronic portfolios, there remain some pivotal questions about their use in the classroom. Such questions as "How can I minimize storage requirements?" dominate any discussion about electronic portfolios. This article examines some of these fundamental questions by using examples from Learning Quest's *Electronic Portfolio* software for the Macintosh platform, and provides practical suggestions toward their successful resolution.

WHICH WORK SAMPLES SHOULD BE INCLUDED IN A STUDENT'S ELECTRONIC PORTFOLIO?

Electronically storing all of a student's work (e.g., handwriting samples, projects, speeches) either by scanning or by cataloging existing documents is both time-consuming and inefficient. As with its text-based counterpart, an electronic portfolio should include only those work samples that best illustrate student success against identified content and performance standards (see

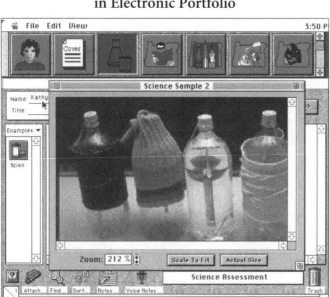

Figure 1
Student Work Sample Suitable for Inclusion
in Electronic Portfolio

the student work sample in Figure 1). According to Engel (1994), Keefe (1995), and Reckase (1995), the selection process should involve shared responsibility between the teacher and student.

We suggest a rather simple process patterned after Oregon's Certificate of Initial Mastery (CIM) portfolio. This process starts with a working or classroom file and culminates with a final electronic portfolio. The working file is stored in a regular file cabinet accessible to students and contains all work completed to date. Prior to a parent conference or the end of a grading period, students select specific items from their working file to be displayed as a showcase portfolio. In Oregon, the showcase portfolio invites students to select items that demonstrate their "can do" skills against the CIM outcomes. Students insert reflection pages as needed, along with their selected work samples. They then bundle the document, either electronically or in text format, into a showcase portfolio containing a reflective introduction, table of contents, reflection pages, and the appropriate showcase work samples.

The final stage is the electronic portfolio. With help from their teacher, students choose the best work from the showcase portfolio and scan or attach their work samples directly into the electronic portfolio. The "attached" student work samples document student performance and can be easily viewed as a *QuickTime* movie, text document, or PICT file. For ease in viewing the final portfolio during a student-led conference, we recommend that the scanned pictures, handwriting samples, video clips, and other items be merged into a *QuickTime* movie or a multimedia presentation using one of the many available multimedia authoring tools (e.g., *Digital Chisel*). In Learning Quest's *Electronic Portfolio* the student's performance can then be scored using a predefined scoring rubric. Following these guidelines for student assessment not only ensures a more efficient portfolio but also frees up space on the computer for those work samples (e.g., scanned images, pictures, word processing, and multimedia documents) that most accurately document student performance. When selecting student work samples, keep in mind that storage requirements vary for different types of documents. Table 1 provides some estimates of storage size for different types of documents.

> **When selecting student work samples, keep in mind that storage requirements vary for different types of documents.**

HOW DO I GET STUDENT WORK SAMPLES INTO THE COMPUTER?

The simplest and most useful way to get work samples into a computer is simply to create the work on a computer. If a document (e.g., movie, picture, graph) already exists in the computer, you can use the electronic portfolio to attach it directly into an existing assessment. Figure 2 shows a sample mathematics assessment and the attached student work samples displayed as icons on the left side of the assessment sheet.

Although it is preferable to create the work on a computer, it is not always feasible. In these situations, one of the following

Table 1	
Student Work Space	*Storage Requirement*
5-page, double-spaced word processing document (no pictures)	45K
Full-page, scanned handwriting sample*	120K
Full-page, scanned black & white picture*	545K
Full-page, scanned color picture*	24,000K (24 Mb)
Quarter-page scanned color picture (300 dpi)*	6,000K (6Mb)
30-second sound clip	300K
15-second QuickTime movie	2,000K (2Mb)

*Actual size varies depending on the resolution, number of colors, and file compression settings used by the scanning software.

Figure 2
Mathematics Assessment with Attached
Student Work Samples

Table 2	
For the best results in...	*Set the scanning resolution to*
Displaying images on the computer screen	72 dpi
Printing images on most laser printers (300 dpi)	150 dpi
Printing images on higher end laser printers (600 dpi)	300 dpi

techniques will be needed to capture and store student work samples on a computer.

Scanning

A scanner can be used to capture any student work that can be photocopied. Scanning works best with documents that have few colors and that do not have much fine detail. Writing samples, hand-drawn pictures, and photographs are examples of student work that can be scanned. Work done in pen will scan better than work done in pencil. When scanning in full color, be aware that images can be huge: 100 megabytes (Mb) or larger! To keep scanned image sizes to a minimum, each item should be scanned at the lowest possible resolution that will still yield acceptable quality.

At a minimum, text on the screen must be readable or the image must be recognizable. Because screen resolution for most Macintosh computers is 72 dots per inch (dpi), this will generally be an optimum resolution for items that are to be viewed only on a computer screen. See Table 2 for tips on getting the highest quality output from a scanned image.

Digitizing Cameras

A digitizing camera, such as the Apple *QuickTake* camera, can be used to capture student work as a digital photograph. Digitizing cameras work best on student work that would traditionally be photographed. Prime candidates for this type of image capture include sculptures, artwork larger than 8.5 × 11", still shots of scenes from a play, before-and-after pictures of an environmental cleanup, and so forth. When loading a digital photograph into Learning Quest's *Electronic Portfolio*, it should be saved as a PICT file. PICT is a universal, generic graphic file format for the Macintosh. One method of presenting a series of still photographs is to combine them into a *QuickTime* movie. *QuickTime* movies function as "mini-slideshows," allowing students and teachers to browse through several work samples at once. The advantage of combining a series of photos into a movie is that *QuickTime* provides very good file compression and cross-platform compatibility. Many freeware or shareware image- and movie-editing tools allow *QuickTime* movies to be created from a series of PICT files.

A Macintosh capable of outputting to videotape can "print" *QuickTime* movies to videotape. This is an excellent way for students to take their portfolio home to show parents, friends, or potential employers.

Video Capture

Many Macintosh computers have the ability to capture video from a VCR or camcorder. These movies can then be saved in *QuickTime* format for playback on any Macintosh or *Windows* computer with *QuickTime* installed. BE WARNED! Full-color, full-screen movies can be extremely large. Thirty seconds of high-quality (no compression), full-screen video can occupy as much as 26Mb of hard disk space. *QuickTime* movies can be stored in a compressed file format that allows long movies to be relatively small in size. *QuickTime* movies can be played back with *SimplePlayer*, or with a variety of other applications that support *QuickTime* movies. The file size of each *QuickTime* movie depends on its duration, size of the image window, and number of colors used.

Black-and-white movies of smaller window sizes and short durations will use the least disk space. Conversely, full-color movies of long durations use the most disk space. Long movies should be shot in or converted to black and white to save space. Reducing the size of the movie window will further reduce file size. The most important factor in the size of *QuickTime* movies is the amount of action taking place in the video sequence. The secret of *QuickTime*'s compressed files is that it stores only the differences between frames. This means that if no changes occur or only minimal changes take place, *QuickTime* can optimize the file size.

Table 3	
Sample QuickTime Movie	*Sample Size*
30 second, black & white, full screen, 4 fps (frames per second), no action	24K
30 second, 8-bit color (256 colors), full screen, 4 fps, no action	50K
1 minute, black & white, full screen, 4 fps, no action	24K
1 minute, 8-bit color, full screen, 4 fps, no action	50K
30 second, black & white, full screen, 4 fps, lots of action	144K
30 second, 8-bit color, full screen, 4 fps, lots of action	488K
30 second, 16-bit color (thousands), full screen, 4 fps, lots of action	976K
30 second, 24-bit color (millions), full screen, 4fps, lots of action	3,456K (3.5Mb)
30 second, 24-bit color, full screen, 30 fps, lots of action	25,920K (26Mb)
30 second, 24-bit color, full screen, 30 fps, lots of action, JPEG compression	1,488 (1.5Mb)

Using the smallest window, fewest number of colors, and greatest amount of compression possible will reduce the amount of hard disk space required for a *QuickTime* movie. For example, a 30-second video clip (normally 26Mb, full screen, with no compression) saved as a quarter-screen movie with compression and 256 indexed colors (instead of millions) will result in a file that is only 2Mb in size. Sample movie sizes for *QuickTime* movies are described in Table 3.

Electronic Portfolio uses the powerful alias facility of the Macintosh System 7 Operating System to keep track of all of its associated files and folders and the devices in which they are stored. This means that *Electronic Portfolio* does not store these items in its database; instead, it stores a special kind of pointer (a file alias) that points to the location of the original file, folder, or storage device. If the original file is moved, the alias will still find it. By using file aliases, *Electronic Portfolio* can find an original item no matter where it gets moved on the disk.

By using file aliases and maintaining only one copy of a folder or file, large amounts of storage space can be saved. This technique is especially useful if a specific file is required on mul-

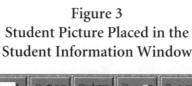

Figure 3
Student Picture Placed in the
Student Information Window

tiple computers connected via a network. Placing the original
on a computer that is accessible to all other computers that may
need it and then placing an alias of the item on each computer
not containing the original is the most effective method of utilizing computer storage space. Aliases can also be used for files
or folders on removable storage media. When items on removable media are accessed through an alias, the operating system
will ask the user to mount the media where the original file is
located.

Minimize Picture Resolutions
Electronic Portfolio allows pictures (PICT format) to be placed
into the Student Information window (see Figure 3) and into
Assessments and/or Reports. However, pictures can require
very large amounts of memory. To minimize the space required
for a picture, the picture must be reduced to the lowest resolution and to the fewest number of colors that will still allow the

original image (on screen) to be recognized. Here are some general suggestions for reducing picture sizes.

1. Scan or save pictures at 72 dpi (screen resolution).
2. Use black-and-white pictures instead of color whenever possible. (They are about 1/12th the size.)
3. Use compression when offered.

WHAT REMOVABLE MASS MEDIA STORAGE DEVICES ARE AVAILABLE?

Electronic Portfolio is designed to use any storage device that can be mounted on the desktop. Any electronic portfolio that attempts to create a well-rounded view of a student will require large amounts of storage. The question then becomes, "How much space will be needed?" We allot 10–15Mb per student per year.

To manage these large storage requirements, it is necessary to use some sort of mass storage device.

To manage these large storage requirements, it is necessary to use some sort of mass storage device. A removable media mass storage device is the most sensible solution because storage requirements for each student grow over time. In most situations, it is not necessary to have older portfolios accessible at all times.

Removable Hard Disks

A removable hard disk is a hard disk that can be easily removed from one computer and attached to another. Removable hard disks commonly use a SCSI (Small Computer System Interface) port to connect to the computer, and they come in a variety of sizes, from 20Mb to 2Gb (1 Gigabyte equals 1,024 Mb). They offer a high degree of reliability and are easy to use but because the drive and the media are the same, the cost per megabyte is high.

Cartridge Drives

A cartridge drive is a storage device that uses removable magnetic disk cartridges for storing the data. Each cartridge encloses an aluminum diskette covered with a microscopic coating of magnetic material. Data is written to and read from the disk by a pair of electromagnetic heads mounted on the ends of radial arms that travel just above and below the disk's surface. There are currently a number of these drives on the market, but the most popular are SyQuest and Iomega (sometimes called a Bernoulli drive). The Iomega drives use cartridges that contain disks coated with magnetic material; however, these disks are made of a flexible plastic similar to that used for floppy disks. These drives come in two sizes and have a variety of storage capacities. They are quite common and are used extensively in the graphic design and desktop publishing fields. They offer a high degree of reliability, a relatively fast access speed, and a low media cost.

Magneto-Optical Drives

A magneto-optical drive is a storage device that uses a removable cartridge that contains a plastic disc with metal particles embedded in its surface. The drive writes data to a given spot on the disc by using a laser on one side of the disc and a high-intensity electromagnet on the other. An intense laser pulse momentarily heats a sector of the disk to a temperature that allows the drive's electromagnet to influence the area's magnetic polarity. This method of storing data on a disk makes stored media much less susceptible to damage and increases the shelf storage life. Magneto-optical drives come in a variety of storage capacities (128/230/650Mb and 1.3Gb). These drives are most common in the graphic design and desktop publishing fields. They offer a very high degree of reliability and a relatively low media cost; however, their access speed is noticeably slower than that of a hard disk.

Recordable CD-ROM Drives (CD-R)

A CD-R drive is a storage device that uses CD-ROM disks for storing the data. They are different from standard CD-ROM drives in that they not only have the ability to play CD-ROM disks but they also have the lasers necessary to burn information onto them. CD-R drives come in a variety of storage capacities and can store up to 650Mb. These drives are most common in the interactive CD-ROM and information service fields. They offer a very high degree of reliability and a low media cost; however, the access speed is noticeably slower than that of a hard disk.

DAT Tape Drives

A DAT tape drive stores data on a 4mm or 8mm Digital Audio Tape (DAT). With built-in data compression and high data-transfer speeds, these drives are the storage device of choice for schools wanting an inexpensive backup system. Recently, Optima Technology® introduced a software package called *DeskTape*. *DeskTape* allows a DAT tape to be mounted in the Finder, as if it were a hard disk. It is now possible to access a DAT tape as if it were a hard disk.

HOW CAN I REDUCE DATA ENTRY TIME?

The two most efficient ways to reduce data entry time are: (1) limit students' work samples to those that adequately reflect and document their "can do" performance and (2) shift the burden of portfolio maintenance from teacher to student. This will help reduce data entry time because less time will be needed for scanning documents, importing pictures, and/or attaching work samples. Establishing an alias for student folders within the electronic portfolio will enable students to update their own folders electronically without the need for teacher intervention.

Several of the options within *Electronic Portfolio* can aid in reducing data entry time. *Electronic Portfolio*'s import/export capability (see Figure 4), for example, allows district or building site personnel to import all student information (e.g., names, parent contacts, emergency phone numbers, standardized test scores) directly into each teacher's Macintosh computer from a district, county, or regional database. An additional option, called Propagate, lets teachers replicate any personal or assessment information within the electronic portfolio for any or all students in the student register. This means that a project description or an assessment for one student can be replicated automatically for an entire class or school without the mundane task of entering information one record at a time. Sharing assessments and reports with other colleagues at a school or throughout a district can further reduce time spent entering data. Once an assessment or report has been created, it can be copied to any other computer running *Electronic Portfolio*.

External hardware devices, including Personal Digital Assistants (PDAs) and barcode readers, can also reduce entry time. Such devices allow teachers the flexibility to assess student

Figure 4
Student Information Accessible with Electronic
Portfolio's Import/Export Option

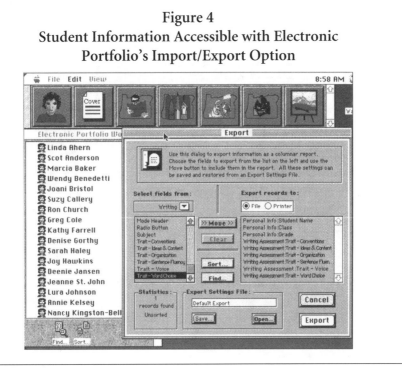

performance without being tethered to the computer. Using the Videx TimeWand I barcode reader and Learning Quest's *EP Barcode* software, teachers can easily create and print barcodes for students and assessments with the click of a button (see Figure 5). With this technology, teachers can literally walk around a classroom or out on the playground assessing student behavior/performance.

CONCLUSION

From a technological perspective, the future of electronic portfolios appears bright. Improvements in mass storage devices, processing speed, and compatibility among various platforms have signaled a new generation of electronic portfolios capable of fulfilling their promise of providing a seamless assessment scheme for K–12 educators. Learning Quest's *Electronic Portfolio* is one such tool that enables classroom teachers to assess, manage, store, and access student portfolios electronically.

Figure 5
Barcode Feature Helps Assess Student Performance

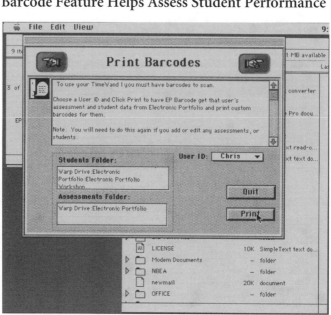

However, their tenure as a viable assessment tool will depend to a large degree on the depth and breadth of the experiences (e.g., open-ended assessment tasks) used to document student attainment of specific outcomes. It is therefore a necessity that serious attention be given to staff development that showcases successful strategies for using electronic portfolios and models exemplary practices for developing authentic assessments that measure all dimensions of a student's academic progress.

REFERENCES

Engel, Brenda S. (1994, Fall). Portfolio assessment and the new paradigm: New instruments and new places. *Educational Forum, 59,* 22–27.

Keefe, Charlotte Hendrick. (1995, Winter). *Portfolios: Mirrors of learning. Council of Exceptional Children, 27,* 66–67.

Reckase, Mark D. (1995, Spring). Portfolio assessment: A theoretical estimate of score reliability. *Educational Measurement: Issues and Practice,* pp. 12–14, 31.

Software
Electronic Portfolio. Learning Quest, Inc., PO Box 61, Corvallis, OR 97339; 800-742-6232.

Technology-Supported Portfolio Assessment

by Helen C. Barrett

T he technology to support alternative assessment is beginning to appear on the market. As we review some of the
commercial software available to support alternative assessment, a few questions should be kept in mind:

• What if teachers, parents, and students could have immediate access to many examples of student work throughout
that student's school years?

... not just paper and pencil work

... including performance
assessments

... including audio and video samples (multimedia)

• What if teachers could streamline the process of acquir-
ing and storing anecdotal observations of student learning?

• Who owns the work that students place into a traditional
portfolio (an ever-growing file folder)?

• How can a teacher manage innovative assessment techniques on top of everything else?

• Can information technologies make classroom assessment easier, not more work for everyone?

A VISION

A good assessment system allows students and teachers to have
a shared understanding of what constitutes good work. Assessment is a lever for school reform and is grounded in shared values. According to Karen Sheingold of the Educational Testing
Service, assessment is a social process that is grounded in:

From *The Computing Teacher,* vol. 21, no. 6 , March 1994, pp. 9–12. © 1994 by
the International Society for Technology in Education. (Updated by Helen C.
Barrett, September 1995.) Reprinted with permission.

- Conversations about student work as evidence of accomplishment
- Development of common language for discussing accomplishments
- Development of shared values and transparent criteria for evaluating student work

According to Sheingold, technology support in assessment allows students and teachers:

1. To make work in many media accessible, portable, examinable, and widely distributable
2. To make performance replayable and reviewable; it is important to see more than once (a video portfolio has been proposed for National Board of Teaching Standards)
3. To address ownership issues

Sam Meisels of the University of Michigan has developed the *Work Sampling System* (pre-K through third grade), which contains the following three components: Performance-Based Checklists, a Portfolio, and a Summary Report. Checklists indicate children's strengths and weaknesses while helping teachers create goals for portfolios. Portfolios inform teachers about the quality of students' work as documented in the checklists. Summary reports, completed three times a year, summarize the checklist and portfolios by translating them into easily understood terms. While Meisels has not incorporated technology into his system, he provides a framework for evaluating potential systems.

SOFTWARE REVIEWS

In 1991, I conducted a research project for the Alaska Department of Education Office of Data Management, exploring a variety of software and hardware options for supporting alternative assessment. Below is a summary of some of the software that I explored and have shared with teachers in subsequent staff development courses and workshops in Alaska and the Pacific Northwest. It should be noted that virtually all of the software reviewed here is for the Macintosh. Most of the software that has been developed and demonstrated at the NECC

93 conference in Orlando was for the Macintosh. Other companies are developing portfolio systems for the MS-DOS/Windows platform: at AERA, NCS conducted a focus group on their prototype system. Several integrated learning systems also include a portfolio component. This article is not meant to be comprehensive but to provide educators with information about available software, hardware, and potential scenarios.

Grady Profile

The *Grady Profile* is the first multimedia software package that I reviewed, primarily because the authors thoughtfully provided a "demo" version that I could explore and give away to teachers. The only difference between the demo version and the real program is the ability to add new students. The *Grady Profile* maintains portfolio information on a Macintosh computer through a set of <u>HyperCard</u> stacks. There is an "early language" version that Apple adapted and has bundled with their Early Language package. This updated version of the *Profile* includes additional assessment in speaking and listening, plus space for both parent and student feedback on the work. Many of these changes were incorporated into the later versions of the commercially-available program.

The program is password protected on initial access, but once into the program, any student's file can be read. The current version offers 15 different screens already designed, plus five cards that the user can define. One of these screens allows students to record reading samples using the Macintosh microphone or the MacRecorder (for older Macs). Another screen allows scanning a student's handwritten work. The latest version allows viewing a *QuickTime* video sample (which must be created by another program).

Almost every screen has a checklist which can be customized by the user, and that can record teacher, parent, and student assessment of each item. A variety of reports can also be created from the data and printed from your favorite word processor.

The *Grady Profile* is the most developed program available on the market today, although it lacks some "user friendliness." It is also missing some features that fit with new thinking on assessment (for example, its math assessment is a skills checklist, which could be improved by scanned examples of problem solving).

Aurbach and Associates are very receptive to suggestions for program revision and are training a group of teacher-trainers. The manual is complete and easy to read and Aurbach produces a semiannual newsletter for registered users. For the teacher wanting to begin, this program provides a comprehensive first step that can be implemented on any Macintosh with *Hyper-Card*. A major enhancement to this program should be available by the time you read this article.

> **One element of assessment is recording anecdotal observations of student learning.**

Learner Profile

One element of assessment is recording anecdotal observations of student learning. Many teachers learned to use "sticky notes" or 3×5 cards that can be stored in student file folders. In Canada, the Victoria Learning Society created a management system for maintaining teachers' anecdotal observations of student work, using bar code technology. The program's designer had a brainstorm while waiting in a grocery store checkout line. What would happen if teachers could use this technology as a form of "shorthand" to record, store, and print out their observations?

The program operates in three stages: planning, observing, and reporting. At the beginning of the observation period, the teacher prints out a page of bar codes, containing a seating chart (with a separate bar code for each student), a set of bar codes for the behaviors that the students were expected to exhibit on that day, qualifiers for those observations, and attendance codes. The teacher observes students working, strokes across a bar code for the student, and strokes across the behavior observed. The current program uses a Videx credit-card-sized optical reader that can later be dropped into an interface box which is connected to a Macintosh. The data is organized by a relational database for later editing and summarizing by student or class or observed behaviors.

The Greater Victoria School District has published several papers about the research used to design their system. I have also seen a videotape that demonstrates the system in use in several classrooms.

Wings for Learning has purchased the *Learner Profile* from Victoria, and has a beta version of the software available. A single user version is available for under $1,000, too high for the average classroom, but multiple bar code readers can be purchased ($350), and two will fit in each docking station.

Chalkboard

The Association for Supervision and Curriculum Development (ASCD) Curriculum Technology Resource Center has published *Chalkboard 1.0,* a program of Macintosh or Windows that allows teachers and students to create multimedia presentations. While not specifically a portfolio program, it does allow the user to assemble a variety of documents into a presentation. *Electronic Chalkboard* creates "hooks" or pointers to various types of files which, with the exception of text, cannot be created within the program. There are two different modes: create and present. The various tools allow access to six different types of media: (1) create or import plain ASCII text files (which can be formatted within the program); (2) play (but not record) sound files; (3) display (but not scan) graphics files; (4) play *QuickTime* movies; (5) create a bar code that can be printed and used to control an optical disk; and (6) create a link to another *Chalkboard* file.

While the program is relatively easy to use, aside from text editing and creating a bar code, there is no way to create the other resources from within the Macintosh version (1.01) that I reviewed. Users must know how to create a sound file with their Macintosh system, to scan graphics files, and to create their own *QuickTime* movies. The documentation is very minimal and does not explain how to create these last three types of files. As a presentation tool for someone who already knows how to use the multimedia features of a personal computer, it could be useful. However, the features are not automated enough for the novice educator. This software has promise, especially if newer versions would include the ability to record sound from within the group, which is on their upgrade list.

Scholastic's Portfolio Product

At NECC 93 in Orlando, Scholastic held several focus group sessions on a prototype electronic portfolio kit that they are looking into developing. Based on their *Point of View* software engine, the program has both a teacher planning component and a student component, and is organized as a timeline. The software appears to be relatively easy to use.

According to Scholastic, the goal of this product would be to provide schools with an easy to use organizational system to facilitate the creation, management, and presentation of performance-based electronic multimedia student portfolios. The application will be a flexible structure containing guides, models, and templates for constructing and accessing activities and portfolios that may be used as is or in a modified, customized form.

The program is being redesigned from the original prototype developed by two creative educators in Vermont, who took the *Point of View* program and have used it with K–12 students as well as student teachers.

KidPix

A few educators are using the *KidPix* program from Brøderbund to develop and maintain young student portfolios. The ability to record and play sound, plus the slide show feature of the *KidPix Companion* program, give younger students a powerful, easy to use software environment.

DATABASE PROGRAMS

More school districts are using database programs to create their own files, especially checklists of student outcomes. Claris provided a template for a student portfolio record system for its *ClarisWorks* program in its publication, *ClarisWorks for Teachers*. One school district in Alaska has developed a complex database template for Claris' *FileMaker Pro* to maintain Chapter 1 and Special Education student records. These programs take time to develop, but can be easily customized and aggregated to meet a district's assessment and reporting needs.

HYPERMEDIA PROGRAMS

Many schools are using various hypermedia programs to maintain student portfolios: *HyperCard, HyperStudio, Asymetrix Toolbox,* and *LinkWay.* With appropriate versions, all of these programs allow incorporation of recorded sound, imported or created text, scanned or created graphics, and will play movie files for teachers who know how to use these programs. However, the level of skill required to take advantage of these capabilities makes this option out of reach for the average teacher in today's classrooms. Another school district in Alaska developed a customized *HyperCard* stack for primary teachers to maintain anecdotal records.

VIDEO PORTFOLIOS

Much work of students, especially in whole language classrooms, is not strictly in written form. With the current emphasis on speaking and listening, as well as writing and reading, any discussion of technology support for student portfolios should include videotape recordings. A lot of schools maintain videotape portfolios of student work.

> If a technology-supported portfolio is to be useful to parents and students, it needs to be in a form that can be easily accessed.

If a technology-supported portfolio is to be useful to parents and students, it needs to be in a form that can be easily accessed. The real advantage of this type of record is the widespread prevalence of video cassette recorders both at home and in schools. According to the Electronic Industries Association, in the early 1990s, only 29% of all homes have a computer, whereas 97% of homes have a color television, 74% have a VCR, and 59% have cable TV. Figures were not available for video cameras in the home, but most classrooms in our state have access to a VCR and a video camera. Therefore, a video record of student presentations would be very feasible to record with currently available technology.

TECHNOLOGY STORAGE CONSIDERATIONS

There are a variety of considerations that need to be addressed when deciding to implement technology support for alternative assessment. Of primary concern is the form that the student data will take as it is stored in digital form. There are different types of files that can be stored, with wide variation in space requirements.

• Application files (the least amount of space on a disk): A two page document = 5K of diskette space.

• Hypermedia files: A normal stack with graphics and text takes up more than 100K on a disk with no sound.

• Scanned graphics: Depending on the file format, a one page file could fill up to 500K.

• Sound files: Depending on the compression ratio, a 30 second sound bite could take up to 100K. (An audio cassette tape would be preferable for storing student work in the "working" portfolio.)

• Movie files: Depending on the compression ratio, a 5 second *QuickTime* file would take over 500K on a disk. (This makes it important to use standard video tapes to maintain the vast majority of full motion video, being very selective about which items to digitize.)

Future Scenarios
Let's envision what the final product might be like and how it might be used. Here are several possible scenarios for electronically creating and storing student portfolios.

Keep a working portfolio
Maintain samples of student work on floppy disk, hard disk drive, removable media drive, or a network. These records could take the following formats:

• scanned images of student handwriting or art
• digitized sound of student reading, digitized with microphone
• standard word processing, database, spreadsheet, or hypermedia files

Maintain a videotape record of student presentations or performances
A low-cost alternative could be an audio cassette recorder. In this format, the classroom teacher works with normal class-

room equipment (a desktop computer, a video camera, or a tape recorder) and accumulates a variety of materials on each student.

Teachers could record anecdotal observations, possibly using the *Learner Profile* system, using bar code technology. A lower cost solution (with a higher time commitment) might be setting up a database for teachers to keep track of student outcomes.

Develop a formal portfolio

The growing need for mass quantities of recordable storage brings about another question: What if teachers, students, and parents had access to modern optical storage to keep copies of student work? At end of each year, students and teachers could select sample files and sample video to place on a writable CD.

Using video compression technology, the best clips from the videotape could be placed in a permanent collection and recorded on a compact disc. Transfer other files to the CD (samples from word processing, hypermedia files, and other applications). The only limitation on this type of storage is the current limitation on accessing the information on a single hardware platform.

FUTURE HARDWARE OPTIONS
CD-R

The education world needs a low-cost compact disc recorder that creates a standard CD that can be read with any multi-session CD-ROM drive. There are CD recorders on the market in the $4,000 price range. This may be too expensive for a single school, but would be reasonable at the district level.

Kodak PhotoCD

Kodak has developed CD technology that allows photographic quality images to be digitized and saved on a specially-formatted compact disc. Up to 50 high quality photographs can be recorded on a single CD. As Kodak develops educational applications for its *PhotoCD*, student work can be transferred from slides to CD for viewing through video (television screen) or computer compact disc players.

CURRENT HARDWARE RECOMMENDED

Apple's AV computers are ideal for portfolios since they include both video input from any video source and will allow video output of computer screens to tape for students to take home. A hand-held scanner or flat bed scanner is needed to integrate paper-and-pencil work into the computer. A microphone or MacRecorder is needed to input student speaking or reading. Other useful hardware devices include:

- Still video camera
- Camcorder
- Video compression board (Video Spigot or ComputerEyes RT)
- Mass storage device such as Bernoulli or Syquest removable media drive or the new ZIP drives (hold 100 Mb)

CONCLUSIONS

Using technology to support alternative assessment is a real possibility with existing technology, and more sophisticated technology is being developed. Teachers can start simply, by keeping student files on floppy or hard disks, and keeping student performances on videotape. Once the technology is available at a reasonable cost, the data can be digitized and placed on the more dense storage medium of the writable optical compact disc. Some day, students will graduate from each level (elementary, middle, and high schools) with a compact disc that contains an entire portfolio.

This article raises more questions than answers, as the technology is just beginning to appear in classrooms. For the next few years, a variety of new programs will appear, giving classroom teachers the opportunity to test out various programs with students. We need a forum to share our mutual experiences so that educators can help shape the technology of assessment for the future. Formative evaluation in this field is very much needed.

[Current updates of this article and other information on student portfolios can be found on the World Wide Web at http://transition.alaska.edu/www/portfolios.html.]

REFERENCES

Sheingold, K. (1992, June). Presentation at a conference on Technology & School Reform, Dallas, TX.

Meisels, S. (1993, June). Presentation at National Head Start Public School Transition Consortium meeting.

Software
Grady Profile—Aurbach & Associates

Learner Profile—Sunburst/Wings for Learning

Chalkboard—ASCD (Association for Supervision & Curriculum Development)

HyperCard, ClarisWorks—Claris Corporation

HyperStudio—Roger Wagner Productions

✓ *KidPix, KidPix Companion*—Brøderbund

Electronic Portfolio—Scholastic

Hardware Peripherals
Paper Port—Visioneer

Quick Cam gray scale video camera—Connectix

Zip Drive—Iomega

The Message: Perusing Portfolios

The growth of the human mind is still high adventure, in many ways, the highest adventure of all.—Norman Cousins

The word *peruse* is defined as "to read or examine, especially with great care." Perusing portfolios simply means that carefully examining portfolios is part of the total process of portfolio development. As the student peruses the portfolio with peers, parents, or teachers, assessment of growth and development is scrutinized. By examining carefully, or perusing, the portfolio, attention is given to the progress the student has made as evidenced by the artifacts and the accompanying reflections. Without this phase of portfolio development in place, the process itself is incomplete. Portfolios, by their very nature, are created with an audience in mind. The opportunity to share the information with others enriches the whole experience.

To fully explore this important aspect of portfolio assessment, five selections are included, ranging from conferencing issues to the ultimate goal of student self-assessment. Each piece has been chosen for its insights into the various aspects of perusing, or "examining with care," the evidence contained in the portfolio.

Leslie Ballard documents her use of portfolios as an English teacher, illustrating the perusal of portfolios as the basis for a final exam. The process is divided into three parts: students rank their artifacts in order of the most effective to the least effective, discuss what they have learned about writing, and end with a description of how they feel about writing. The final papers meet set criteria for an essay format and are submitted for a final grade. The students' entries seemed to verify that they have great insight into their own strengths and weaknesses; they referred to the power of peer editing and presented honest expressions of their meaningful learning. In addition, the teacher gains insight into his or her teaching through the students' comments, and the students seem to embrace the rigorous self-assessment model.

In another example of how the perusal of portfolios enhances the learning process, Vincent J. Melograno articulates how students are motivated to learn in K–12 physical education classes by reflecting on items in the portfolio that evidence their skills, understandings, social behaviors, and values. Delineating the whole process of portfolio development, the evaluation stage is highlighted with the use of specific observation checklists, peer reflections, and parent conferences.

In an even more comprehensive piece, F. Leon Paulson and Pearl R. Paulson present student-led conferences from the preparation stage through the conference itself. In this informative discussion, they address teacher concerns about how to manage the conference, as well as other issues such as student motivation. Particular schools, already implementing portfolio conferences, are also mentioned, as well as a complete vignette from a middle school documenting the process from beginning to end.

Complementing the two pieces on perusing portfolios through the use of parent conferences is a Vermont State Department of Education document targeted to parents. Entitled "Portfolios and Your Child: Some Questions and Answers for Parents and Families," this article presents information in a user-friendly format of basic parent questions followed by helpful answers that are peppered with specific examples. Particular attention is given to guiding parents toward skillful examination of the portfolio, including insightful comments on what they might see and how they might interpret what is there. In addition, there are useful ideas about what parents and family members can actually do to help the child.

The final selection in this section is a particularly rich piece by Elizabeth A. Hebert that suggests that reflection is invited with the use of portfolios, not only by the students, but by the staff as well. Highlighted in the essay are two specific techniques that are used in one school to make the assessment more meaningful. Both "Learning Experience Forms" and "Portfolio Evenings" receive attention from Hebert. Not only do students become better at assessing their learning, but teachers feel they are part of a more empowered, effective faculty.

With this final piece, the case for perusing portfolios is made. The reading or examination with care is, after all, what the true purpose of portfolios is all about. Herein lies their power to enhance the learning process.

Portfolios and Self-Assessment

by Leslie Ballard

U sing portfolios as a teaching tool or as an assessment device continues to provide food for discussion inside and outside the English classroom. At the secondary level, standard portfolio use does not always seem to be practical given the constraints of producing hard evidence of achievement at given intervals.

My first experience with portfolios simply involved keeping all of the students' writing in folders and passing them on to their next English teacher. This was an effort to keep track (on the teachers' part) of the students' progress and also to try to stem plagiarism problems. However, with large classes it was not always possible for the teacher to sit down and read through the folders, and the students were never called upon to assess their progress in writing through reviewing their folders.

When I began teaching an advanced composition class of high-school seniors, I automatically began to keep the students' papers. They could review them at any time and take them home while working on another assignment, so they could benefit from the comments. Upon discovering that a final examination for the course was required, I was stumped. The students write some timed in-class essays, but I have always been unhappy with the idea of using that for a final, and a multiple-choice exam over the basics of writing has never appealed to me. So, as an experiment, I decided to use the portfolios as the basis for the final examination to give the students a chance to assess their own writing and their progress.

From *English Journal,* vol. 81, no. 2, February 1992, pp. 46–48. © 1992 by the National Council of Teachers of English. Reprinted with permission.

The assignment involved three steps:

1.   The students rank their papers in order of most to least effective with a brief rationale for what they think are the good and bad points and what they have learned through the assignment.

2.   They discuss what they have learned about writing as a result of this course and the way they go about writing.

3.   They describe how they feel at this point about writing and how they view writing now as opposed to before taking the course.

My criteria for the final papers were as follows: they adhere to standard essay format, avoid a critique of the instructor (to prevent a last minute, desperate bid for points), and practice honesty. Students could determine the length. They would take their portfolios home with them over a weekend and then have two class periods to write their papers. They could bring in notes, but the writing was to be done in class.

> **I did not know what to expect when I first gave this assignment, and the students, while intrigued, were a bit suspicious.**

I did not know what to expect when I first gave this assignment, and the students, while intrigued, were a bit suspicious. No length requirement? They were to assess what they had written? What if they did not agree with me? They were not to mention my name? How would they go about organizing their papers? How would these papers be graded? After I had allayed their fears as best I could and offered advice about possible organizational methods they might use, they took their folders with them. They trudged out the door, still viewing me with some suspicion.

The group was a mixed one with some students taking the class for college credit and others because they were coerced by parents or counselors. Their abilities were mixed as well. So my expectations were that the stronger students would naturally do a better job, and the weaker writers would hand in their typical efforts. I was quite wrong.

Reading the finals in the teachers' lounge, I was amazed by, and pleased with, this experiment. The other teachers wondered how I could be having such a good time grading a final.

The first thing that struck me was their insight into their own strengths and weaknesses and their willingness to be honest about their efforts. Invariably, I agreed with the students and their reasons for ranking their papers although they tended to be more critical of themselves than I was of them. When discussing their good and bad points, they used the vocabulary of composition. They seemed to realize the importance of focus, logic, and coherence, and they were especially concerned with the need to express their ideas as smoothly as possible. Most pleasing to me in this phase was their ability to look at their essays without being bound by my comments and evaluation.

> **The first thing that struck me was their insight into their own strengths and weaknesses.**

They did not mimic the comments I had written on their papers, but told what they learned from particular assignments, ranging from technical problems (overcoming sentence structure errors, organizing material more effectively, developing ideas more fully) to more personal insights. Many commented on how they finally realized how important thinking was at every step of the process ("from this experience, I learned that thinking things through before scribbling pays off" and "this essay has taught me things about myself and how I feel that I should have known a long time ago"). Since the majority of the students were confirmed procrastinators at the beginning of the course, I read many comments about that failing. Some realized early in the course the dangers of putting off their writing until the last minute, and their progress reflected that. Others didn't but swore mighty oaths that they had learned the hard way and would never do it again. (Only their college professors will know for sure!)

What they learned about writing usually included how difficult it is ("I always thought that it was easy to write, but I was wrong. Putting words on paper and writing are two different things"). They also learned what a joy it can be on those seemingly rare occasions when everything falls into place. It was interesting to note the different strategies they tried during the process. Writer's block became less and less of a problem as the course continued, and they seemed to enjoy experimenting with the different strategies to overcome it.

The helpfulness of peer critiques was frequently cited. We use a variety of methods ranging from anonymous free responses at the beginning of the semester to group responses and one-on-one conferencing. The students found that looking critically at others' writing made them more critical of their own. They liked getting feedback on passages they were happy with and on those that had given them problems. Often they were surprised by their readers' interpretation of their work and afterward willingly spent time creating the desired impact. As one young woman observed, "I have found that language in the written sense will work for you if you take time with it."

> **They had begun to view themselves as writers rather than as students enrolled in a composition course.**

Almost unanimous was the realization of the benefits of revision. Their self-assessments were honest, and they recognized that in the beginning of the course they were really editing, if that, rather than making substantive revisions. They saw that the quality of the papers that had not been revised at least once was not what they had come to demand of themselves by the end of the semester. It was heartening to read their comments about revision.

> Now, I am my own number one critic.
> I have learned that one draft will never be enough.
> Writing may be a gift, but writing well is an accomplishment.

The section describing their feelings about themselves as writers was the most interesting part of the essay. They had begun to view themselves as writers rather than as students enrolled in a composition course. Many noted the confidence they now felt regardless of their grade—a readiness to try any type of writing. One writer noted that "this confidence motivated me to progress" while another mentioned that "I feel more at ease and more relaxed which in turn helps me to write better." Others, however, did not share this feeling, some having never written a full-fledged essay. One writer confessed that she "really didn't learn much about writing. . . . If I have to write, I want to write the way I want to since that is the easiest way for me to write."

From this final, I learned quite a bit about myself as a teacher of writing and benefited from many of the comments in terms of improving the course. But what I liked most was the authority behind these essays. The students may not have accomplished what they wanted, although their expectations and standards had risen quite a bit during the course, or received the grades that they wanted, but they all seemed to know what they were talking about. As I watched them write those two days, I realized I had seldom seen students write with such intensity. Students who always complained about trying to come up with five hundred words were suddenly writing four to seven pages when no length requirement was imposed. Others whose writing had been plagued throughout the semester with mechanical errors handed in papers with few if any such problems.

Not all was rosy. Some students were bitter about grades or penalties for not handing in papers. A few showed little or no insight into themselves or the process of writing. But over the course of four semesters of using this final, I have found these exceptions to be rare. Instead, I read more and more about students waking to the joy that is inspired by becoming an adept writer: "Writing is a world of magic. In one paper you can make your reader see and experience what only you have experienced. . . . I have grown to appreciate the art of writing."

The students' oral comments as they handed in their papers were also enlightening. Several said that this was such a refreshing final; they did not have to memorize formulas or dates, but they believed as a result they had really learned something they thought of as significant. It truly seemed to be a final that not only reflected the course but also gave my students an opportunity to reflect about their learning.

Portfolio Assessment: Documenting Authentic Student Learning

by Vincent J. Melograno

The 1980s saw a demand for greater educational effectiveness. Since publication of *A Nation at Risk* (National Commission on Excellence in Education, 1983), there has been much legislation and numerous education projects directed toward curriculum reform and school restructuring (Kohl, 1992; Levine & Ornstein, 1993). More recently, *America 2000: An Education Strategy* (U.S. Department of Education, 1991) emphasized the key elements needed to ensure widespread educational reform. This vision of American education, including a set of national goals, led to passage of the Goals 2000: Educate America Act (PL 103-227) in March 1994. One result of the reform movement is the focus on student outcomes—clearly developed, publicly stated outcomes that are linked to learning units and assessment. The Physical Education Outcomes Project (Franck et al., 1992) is consistent with this focus. Its unified guide includes outcome statements and grade-level "benchmarks" (competencies) which amplify the definition of the physically educated person.

The need for school improvement and accountability relative to student learning has never been more evident. Interest in assessment has also been prompted by accountability concerns, especially the need to organize classroom data in ways that are credible and comprehensible to all constituencies—student,

From *Journal of Physical Education, Recreation, and Dance*, vol. 65, no. 8, October 1994, pp. 50–55, 58–61. © 1994 by the American Alliance for Health, Physical Education, Recreation, and Dance, 1900 Association Drive, Reston, VA 22091. Reprinted with permission.

teacher, parent, and community. Although society has been oriented toward standardized achievement tests, there is an apparent readiness for change. Alternatives include more naturalistic, performance-based approaches to assessment. While these approaches are intended to promote a better alignment of instruction and assessment, they entail new roles for teachers and students in the evaluation process (Chittenden, 1991). However, in physical education, these roles may not be entirely new since a performance-based approach coincides with what is typically evaluated (e.g., motor abilities, sports skills, games, strategies, fair play).

> **Although society has been oriented toward standardized achievement tests, there is an apparent readiness for change.**

Developing a systematic evaluation procedure does not mean the group-administered, objectively scored, and normative interpretation of achievement tests. Rather, a comprehensive, performance-based measure of learning is recommended that documents not only understandings and skills, but other outcomes such as attitudes, motivations, social conduct, and values. Evaluation which scans this full spectrum of student learning reflects the trend towards "authentic assessment" (Perrone, 1991).

In authentic assessment, examples of student performances, not the highly inferential estimates provided by group testing, are used to measure learning (Meisels, 1993). For example, in physical education students' performances in naturalistic game settings (e.g., volleyball bump pass is rated when returning a "real" serve) are assessed instead of the results of a skill test (e.g., volleyball bump pass is rated from a partner lob). This notion is also basic to the sport education model (Siedentop, 1994), in which student performance is authentically related to class goals (e.g., seasonal performances, execution of gymnastics routines in competition, weight training performance records).

Authentic assessment is an ongoing feedback system which documents student learning through exhibits and work samples inherent to the school setting. It is nonstigmatizing, enhances motivation, assists teachers with decision making, and is effective for reporting accomplishments and progress to parents. Traditional grades may be replaced with anecdotal records, performance samples, and student profiles. The various forms of authentic assessment seem to have common goals: (1) to capitalize on the actual work of students; (2) to enhance teacher and student involvement in evaluation; and (3) to satisfy the accountability need prompted by school reform (Chittenden, 1991). Further-

> **Portfolio assessment is designed to present a broader, more genuine picture of student learning.**

more, these performance-based assessments can be longitudinal (i.e., across grade levels), multidimensional (i.e., physical, intellectual, social, and emotional), and individually modifiable (i.e., wide range of learner variability) (Meisels et al., 1993).

This broadened view of assessment coincides with holistic approaches to teaching such as "whole language" and "developmentally appropriate" practice (Viechnicki et al., 1993), including recommended practice in physical education. With respect to assessment, developmentally appropriate practice in physical education means that, "Teacher decisions are based primarily on ongoing individual assessments of children as they participate in physical education class activities (formative evaluation), and not on the basis of a single test score (summative evaluation)" (Graham et al., 1992, p. 7).

While there are many authentic assessment techniques, portfolios are emphasized as the primary way of exhibiting student work and performance data. Portfolio assessment is designed to present a broader, more genuine picture of student learning (Zessoules & Gardner, 1991). Although relatively new in education, portfolios have been used for a long time by commercial artists, journalists, architects, photographers, models, and other professionals to showcase achievements and skills. In education, portfolios are used to assess students' strengths and weaknesses over time (DeFina, 1992). They have gained widespread use in reading, writing, art, music, literature, foreign language, and English (Belanoff & Dickson, 1991: Gilbert, 1993).

Portfolio implementation in physical education has begun to emerge. For example, at Southridge Middle School in Fontana, California, "sportfolios" are used for outcome-based education. Fitness progress is tracked, competencies are demonstrated, and student interactive behaviors are rated. Artifacts are collected for individual student's sportfolios (Marmo, 1994). In Orange County, California, technology is used extensively. Computer grading programs with rubrics, motor skills videotapes, computer simulations, and digitized video of pre-post demonstration of skills contribute to "electronic" portfolios (Mohnsen & Thompson, 1994). In Kentucky, authentic performance assessment tasks and the learner outcomes mandated by the Kentucky Education Reform Act of 1990 focus on the students' abilities to produce quality portfolios (Meadors et al., 1994).

The "assessment movement" originated in regular classrooms and other subjects. In this article, general education concepts are applied to physical education since little has been suggested for physical education portfolios. But, the future appears bright given the exemplary use of portfolios in the school settings described. Therefore, the purposes of this article are to:

• describe the essential characteristics of portfolio assessment;

• identify a framework for the development of portfolios;

• examine various aspects of portfolio evaluation; and

• propose a portfolio collection model for physical education.

CHARACTERISTICS OF PORTFOLIO ASSESSMENT

A distinction should be made between assessment and evaluation. Assessment refers to the process of gathering and organizing information or data in ways that make it possible for teachers, students, and/or parents to make judgments. Evaluation refers to examining and interpreting the collected information or data and determining its value. Portfolio assessment, then, is the purposeful and systematic collection of student work that shows individual effort, progress, and achievement in one or more areas of learning. Students must be involved in selecting and judging the quality of their own work, including self-reflection (Paulson, Paulson, & Meyer, 1991).

Benefits

Portfolio assessment offers a dynamic, visual presentation of a student's abilities, strengths, and areas of needed improvement. The benefits are revealed by a comparison between the characteristics of portfolio assessment and what seems to be traditional testing practice (Tierney, Carter, & Desai, 1991). Portfolios: (1) represent a wide range of student work in a given content area; (2) engage students in self-assessment and goal setting; (3) allow for student differences; (4) foster collaborative assessment; (5) focus on improvement, effort, and achievement; and (6) link assessment and teaching to learning. In physical education, these elements have always existed as part of any broad-based assessment process that uses learning data derived from drills, practice, and game settings. Portfolios offer a way to organize and manage these performance results.

Students must be involved in selecting and judging the quality of their own work.

Testing practices usually: (1) cover a limited content area and may not truly represent what students have learned; (2) rely on teacher-scored or mechanically-scored results with little student input; (3) examine all students on the same dimensions; (4) minimize teacher-student and student-student collaboration; (5) address achievement only; and (6) separate assessment, teacher, and learning. In physical education, this has meant end-of-unit skills tests with little relationship to what might have actually been learned.

Teacher's Role

While there are elements of current instructional delivery systems that could foster alternative assessment strategies, changes are needed to implement portfolios in physical education. Traditional teaching roles may not work. For example, in the portfolio model, the teacher facilitates, guides, and offers choices rather than informs, directs, and predetermines priorities. Partnerships are established among teachers, students, and parents. More specifically, teachers would need to:

- plan for student involvement and input;

- provide time for tasks that encourage decision making and reflection;
    - provide for modeling of expectations;
    - help students manage portfolios;
    - develop positive interactive behaviors; and
    - use interactions to guide instruction.

Logistical Considerations

Some teachers will look at portfolio assessment and say, "I have too many students and not enough time." The reality for most teachers is to manage students first and deliver some kind of instruction second. Assessment may be a distant third. However, portfolios demand a high level of student self-responsibility in terms of self-management, self-assessment, self-reflection, and peer conferencing and evaluation. If students gradually learn to use a system of portfolio assessment, restrictions of time and sheer numbers are minimized. Use of partners, small groups, and self-directed tasks can reduce the seemingly high student-teacher ratios. Obviously, the system needs to be well planned and organized, the elements of which are described in this article. Portfolio assessment should be implemented incrementally, starting with appealing aspects and followed by the aspects that complete the system.

> Use of partners, small groups, and self-directed tasks can reduce the seemingly high student-teacher ratios.

DEVELOPMENT OF PORTFOLIOS

A multifaceted approach is recommended for developing portfolios. Ideally, all stakeholders (i.e., student, teacher, parents, community) should be involved in the process; a rationale should exist for including portfolio items; and the purposeful collection of students' work should occur over time. As teachers and students collect portfolio data, progress should be reported at regular intervals to parents, administrators, and others, as appropriate. Portfolios should not be a collection of "anything and everything." Information gathering should be based on multiple methods such as observations, performance samples, and tests or test-like procedures (Chittenden, 1991). The framework for developing portfolios includes the following components.

Purpose

The first consideration in any portfolio system is its purpose. There needs to be a reason for creating portfolios. Imagine the difficulty in selecting items for a portfolio with no sense of what the portfolio is to represent. General purposes include:

- keeping track of student's progress;
- providing students with an opportunity to assess their own accomplishments;
- assisting the teacher in instructional planning;
- determining the extent to which established learning objectives have been achieved;
- helping parents understand their children's effort and progress;
- serving as a basis for program evaluation; and
- determining student placement within and outside of class (Murphy & Smith, 1992).

Purposes specific to physical education might include:

- helping students practice healthy lifestyles;
- determining the degree of personal and social development in an adventure-outdoor education program; and
- communicating students' strengths and weaknesses in gross and fine motor skills.

Organization and Management

First, choose a method of construction (e.g., file folders inside an accordion file, packet folders held together with a spiral binding, hanging files, boxes). Every item should be dated and a cumulative list of items maintained in the front of the portfolios. Second, decide how and where to store portfolios (e.g., milk crates, file cabinets or drawers, shelves, boxes). Portfolios must be stored in locations that are visible and accessible to students. Third, manage portfolios regularly to avoid a large pile of items at the end of a given collection period. And fourth, decide who should have access to portfolios (e.g., peers, parents, other teachers). Certain portfolio sections or items may be designated as public while others are private. Establish guidelines from the beginning.

Item Selection

Usually, students' first portfolio items are "baseline" samples. Contain the information collected through the techniques and sources of entry appraisal (pre-assessment) in students' portfolios. For example, behavior sampling through informal techniques (observations and self-reports) and formal techniques (criterion-referenced measures) yields important baseline information to ultimately show student progress (learning). Other entries, such as cumulative record data (e.g., previous test scores, diagnostic reviews, anecdotal records) and performance on a task sequence, also produce valuable information.

> When selecting the contents of a portfolio, keep in mind two compelling factors—the students' desires and the purpose for collecting each item.

Other criteria are also needed for choosing portfolio items. For example, an item might be selected that represents "something that was hard for you to do," "something that makes you feel really good," and/or "something that you would like to work on again." Additional suggestions includes a "best" or "most representative" skill (e.g., gymnastic stunt), work-in-progress with written plans for revision (e.g., dance routine), and samples organized chronologically according to a theme (e.g., personalized physical fitness program).

Variety of Items

When selecting the contents of a portfolio, keep in mind two compelling factors—the students' desires and the purpose for collecting each item. Portfolios should be student-centered. When students make decisions about the selection and quality of their work, they begin to establish standards by which their work can be evaluated. However, students must realize that teachers will also decide on portfolio items and that some items may be mandated by school officials (DeFina, 1992). Items can include: pre-instruction inventory, journals, task sheets, student reflections, self-assessment checklists, projects, frequency index scales, independent study contracts, rating scales, videotapes, peer reviews, teacher's anecdotes, attitude surveys, parental observations/comments, self-reports, skill tests, workbook pages, quizzes, logs, and written tests.

PORTFOLIO EVALUATION

Given the nature of portfolio assessment, is it really necessary to evaluate portfolios? The answer is yes! Simply collecting items serves no meaningful teaching, learning, or evaluation purpose. If nothing else, portfolios should be linked to established learning objectives. However, many teachers have abandoned conventional symbols—grades and scores—in favor of new ways to evaluate. Instead, they describe, analyze, moderate, discuss, annotate, and conference (Murphy & Smith, 1992). Remember that no single portfolio item should be used to evaluate students' abilities. To draw accurate conclusions, performance patterns should be analyzed over time.

> The portfolio's purpose should help define the type of evaluation as well as the person who will do the evaluating.

The development of criteria and procedures for evaluating portfolios is a challenging task. The portfolio's purpose should help define the type of evaluation as well as the person who will do the evaluating. Teachers should collaborate with students, parents, and other teachers so that expectations are clearly communicated. Several aspects of portfolio evaluation follow.

Reflection

Evaluative criteria are inherent to many portfolio items. As students develop and select their work samples, they become reflective in the process. That is, they make value judgments about the standards being used as a guide to evaluation. Over time, high-order cognitive functions such as analysis and synthesis are promoted. To help strengthen self-reflective abilities, some structure is recommended. For example, at selected intervals, students could be expected to complete a "self-reflective activity sheet," the purposes of which could vary according to:

• *Process and progress.* Questions pertain to a portfolio "audit": What's in stock? How many items do you have? What items are you thinking about? What are you working on? What problems are you having in collecting items? Is your log up to date?

• *Revision.* Questions focus on describing, judging, and selecting appropriate revisions: How would you describe your skill? Your knowledge? Your teamwork? What are some problems you perceive in achieving your desired skill level? What are some changes you can make to deal with these problems?

> Portfolios are excellent ways for parents to see what their children have achieved and are trying to achieve.

• *Setting goals.* Questions relate to past and future goals: What goals did you set for yourself? What items show that you accomplished them? How do you feel about your goals? What are your goals for next month? By the end of the year? (Murphy & Smith, 1992)

Reflections on individual student's portfolios are not limited to self-assessment. Peers can offer valuable feedback. However, they should not merely speculate about another student's performance; they must judge other's work according to established criteria. Reciprocal learning approaches use peer reviews and corresponding checklists or rating scales, items that can be kept in portfolios. A "peer reflection form" can assess a student's overall view of a peer's portfolio with questions such as: What do you see as the special strength of the work? What could be improved? What suggestions would you offer based on your own experiences?

Parents can also provide feedback and support. Portfolios are excellent ways for parents to see what their children have achieved and are trying to achieve. The more parents and children interact through portfolios, the stronger the home-school connection (Murphy & Smith, 1992). Introduce and explain the portfolio program to parents in a letter or during an open house or "portfolio night." To get parental feedback, distribute a "parent portfolio review and reflection form" with questions such as: Which items tell you most about your child's achievements? What do you see as your child's strengths? What do you see as needs to be addressed? What suggestions do you have for improving your child's performance?

Conferences

Establish a revolving schedule to meet with students to analyze portfolios and evaluation measures. Because of time constraints and logistics, conferences may need to occur while the rest of the students are working independently at stations or in small groups. Address topics such as portfolio organization, item selection, evaluation criteria, and results. Encourage students to discuss their own observations about growth and compare them with your judgments. Devise appropriate plans for improvement and development. Focus on accomplishments and potential growth, not problems or failures. Conferences should not be perceived as teacher inquisitions. Create a "conference questions sheet" to record answers and/or comments to predetermined questions.

In addition, use a "conference evaluation form" to record teacher and student notes. These notes, which become a form of agreement, should be kept in the portfolios. Conferences serve as evaluative measures and become part of the portfolios' anecdotal histories (Clemmons et al., 1993).

Conferences between parents and teachers afford another opportunity to share students' portfolios and to communicate evaluative judgments. Baseline samples should be compared to present samples so parents can see their children's growth. Stated goals should also be compared to targeted areas of improvement. Establish guidelines for parental review so that students know how their parents will be involved and how the collected information will be used (DeFina, 1992).

Progress Reports

Traditional grading systems and report cards are a reality within the educational establishment. Translating portfolio contents into report card grades can be difficult since grades typically rate students on a curve and portfolios place students on a developmental continuum. Also, portfolios are normally skewed in that students' "best" work is usually presented; therefore, a full representative sample of students' actual learning should be assured.

Adaptive techniques can be used to make portfolios complement conventional report card grades. By looking holistically at portfolio items, it is possible to arrange them in A, B, C categories. Rubrics, a scoring guide designed to evaluate a student's performance, can be used for this purpose (Batzle, 1992). For example, a rubric could measure the components of a synchronized swimming routine (i.e., synchronization, creativity, fluidity, and diversity). A rating scale is devised (e.g., range of 0 to 5) with the largest number indicating "outstanding." Criteria are established for each score across each component.

Report cards can be redesigned to include narrative statements and/or descriptive labels, but it may be more practical to supplement report cards with anecdotal progress reports. Progress reports clearly communicate learners' accomplishments, their strengths and difficulties, and their progress. The report shown in figure 1 is based on performance indicators rather than grades. On the reports, progress is judged "as expected" or "not as expected"/ "needs improvement." Space is made for general comments about strengths and weaknesses in each component. Plans for supporting learner growth can also be included.

PORTFOLIO COLLECTION MODEL

Implementing portfolio practices requires a profound shift in the responsibilities and roles of students, teachers, and parents. Students are active participants in the assessment process. Ownership of their development enables them to make use of metacognitive processes as a tool for learning (e.g., self-reflection, teacher-student conferencing, peer critique, and parent-child interaction). They become reflective about the way they think and their thought processes. In other words, they are able to understand why they think and act in a particular way (DeFina, 1992).

Teachers are reflective practitioners. Traditionally, they judge students' work against their own or other mandated standards. Now, they become accomplished facilitators in the process of portfolio self-assessment (Zessoules & Gardner, 1991). Parents are involved partners. They share in the supportive network that includes the link between school and home.

The range of potential "exhibits of learning" contained in an individual portfolio is unlimited. Information gathering methods and the kinds of portfolio items represent a means by

Figure 1. Progress Report for Elementary Students

Student: _____ Teacher: _____ Date: _____

__ 1st qtr. (Nov.)   __ 2nd qtr. (Feb.)   __ 3rd qtr. (April)   __ 4th qtr. (June)

Achieved   Needs Improvement   Working to achieve

Physical
— — — 1. Executes all locomotor movements in response to rhythmic accompaniments.
— — — 2. Controls body while balancing, rolling, climbing, and hanging.
— — — 3. Shows body control in manipulating playground ball while stationary and moving.

Comments: _____

Intellectual
— — — 1. Knows rules and procedures governing movement activities and games.
— — — 2. Recognizes the effects of space, time, force, and flow on the quality of movement.
— — — 3. Applies basic mechanical principles that affect and control human movement.

Comments: _____

Social
— — — 1. Respects rights, opinions, and abilities of others.
— — — 2. Shares, takes turns, and provides mutual assistance.
— — — 3. Participates cooperatively in student-led activities.

Comments: _____

Emotional
— — — 1. Assumes responsibility for giving and following directions.
— — — 2. Makes decisions on an individual basis.
— — — 3. Responds freely and confidently through expressive bodily movement.

Comments: _____

Values
— — — 1. Carries out tasks to completion.
— — — 2. Displays preferences for various forms of movement.
— — — 3. Engages in movement activities voluntarily.

Comments: _____

which portfolio assessment can be guided. Following are brief descriptions of methods and portfolio items, illustrated relative to physical education. Many of the items described are partial in nature. Complete instruments and procedures that correspond to these selected items can be found in other sources (Melograno, 1985, in press).

> Portfolio assessment offers a system that is context-responsive— real learning that is found in naturalistic settings.

Observations (table 1) refers to the kinds of behavior cues that are seen in everyday class activities. Behaviors that show movement abilities, interests, social conduct, and thinking can be recorded through observational formats (e.g., rating forms, checklists, anecdotes).

Performance samples (table 2) refers to tangible products or artifacts representing students' accomplishments. These kinds of formats are not as readily available in physical education settings since learning is usually centered on movement forms rather than "documents." However, there are many samples of performance (e.g., projects, videotapes) that should be considered.

Tests and test-like procedures (table 3) refers to the full range of instruments (e.g., commercial, teacher-designed). "Test" does not necessarily imply formal, teacher-directed procedures. Informal inventories and end-of-unit tasks are valuable in documenting student learning.

Teachers have long known that the time spent on assessment does not always yield the desired educational benefits. We so often hear, "That test didn't really show what she can do!" The inadequacies of standardized, group-based assessment beg for an alternative approach. Portfolio assessment offers a system that is context-responsive—real learning that is found in naturalistic settings. The unique contributions of physical education to students' cognitive, affective, and pyschomotor needs coincides with the underlying philosophy and principles of portfolio assessment.

Table 1. Method of Portfolio Assessment—Observations

Information Source	Illustrative Items (partial)
Rating scales	**Tennis forehand** (1) (2) (3) (4) (5) • contacts ball when even with front foot ❏ ❏ ❏ ❏ ❏ • keeps wrist firm; swings with whole arm from shoulder ❏ ❏ ❏ ❏ ❏ • rotates trunk so hips and shoulders face net on follow through ❏ ❏ ❏ ❏ ❏
Checklists	**Forward roll** Trial 1 Trial 2 Trial 3 • tucks head with chin to chest ❏ ❏ ❏ • shifts body weight forward until off balance ❏ ❏ ❏ • accepts body weight with arms ❏ ❏ ❏

Frequency index scales

Behavior Trends	1st Observation					2nd Observation					Rating Average
	Never	Seldom	Fairly Often	Frequently	Regularly	Never	Seldom	Fairly Often	Frequently	Regularly	
1. Limits interactions to friends; excludes others	5	4	3	2	1	5	4	3	2	1	
2. Shares equipment	1	2	3	4	5	1	2	3	4	5	
3. Takes turn at circuit stations	1	2	3	4	5	1	2	3	4	5	

Information Source	Illustrative Items (partial)
Peer reviews	Partner checks performance according to the criteria **Cartwheel criteria** P A NI • faces mat with preferred foot forward; same-side arm vertical ❏ ❏ ❏ • throws weight upon preferred foot; leans forward, placing same-side hand on mat ❏ ❏ ❏ • throws opposite leg up at the same time, placing same-side hand on mat ❏ ❏ ❏ P = perfect/A = acceptable/NI = needs improvement
Logs	Fitness calendar showing aerobic and strength training workout schedule
Anecdotal recordings	Descriptive statement about student's ability to change direction and levels during movement exploration
Narrative descriptions	Summary of student's progress in developing descriptions [of] cooperative behaviors during a "new games" unit

Table 2. Method of Portfolio Assessment—Performance Samples

Information Source	Illustrative Items (partial)
Self-evaluations	Evaluate own ability according to the criteria **Golf grip criteria (bottom hand)** I have achieved Working to achieve • placed on club first, fingers as close together as possible ❏ ❏ • thumb close to hand at the first joint ❏ ❏ • wrist is directly above shaft ❏ ❏ • thumb forms "V"; forefinger points over opposite shoulder ❏ ❏
Student reflections	Circle the words that describe how you feel (mostly) about gymnastics: Interesting Too easy Useful Others: Dull Helpful Worthless _____ Fun Important Boring _____ Too hard Super Useless _____ Check (✓) the face you wear when you look at this picture:
Projects	**Personalized fitness program:** • Plot a personal physical fitness profile based on ratings. • Generate fitness goals based on ratings. • Select exercise and/or leisure activities in terms of contributions to fitness goals. • Design a program based on goals, activity selection, and activity schedule.
Independent study	**Badminton contract:** • Improve performance in 6 of 8 skills by at least one ability rating. • Use mechanical principles, points of contact, and possible uses of criteria to compare/contrast: (1) overhead clear vs. forehand drive; (2) smash vs. overhead drop; and (3) long serve vs. short serve. • Write a brief report (4–5 pages) on the history of badminton. • Create a test on badminton terms, rules, and strategies; test and grade three classmates.
Videotapes	Free exercise routine; swimming stroke; game play

Table 3. Method of Portfolio Assessment—Tests and Testlike Procedures

Information Source	Illustrative Items (partial)
Pretests	On the diagram, draw diagonal lines to show the area that is used during a singles game in tennis. Place an "X" where the server stands to begin a game, and an "0" where the serve stands when the score is 30–15.
Quizzes	For each pair of descriptions, indicate the associated component. 　　　　　　　　　　　　　　　　Strength　Endurance 1. (a) One maximal contraction　　❏　　　❏ 　 (b) Sustained contraction 2. (a) Light weights, many reps　　❏　　　❏ 　 (b) Heavy weights, few reps 3. (a) Greater hypertrophy　　　　❏　　　❏ 　 (b) Greater capillarization
Self-reports	Check the space that designates how you feel most of the time. Coed volleyball is: <table><tr><td>Exciting</td><td></td><td></td><td></td><td></td><td></td><td></td><td>Dull</td></tr><tr><td>Boring</td><td></td><td></td><td></td><td></td><td></td><td></td><td>Fun</td></tr><tr><td>Worth the time</td><td></td><td></td><td></td><td></td><td></td><td></td><td>Waste of time</td></tr><tr><td>Stupid</td><td></td><td></td><td></td><td></td><td></td><td></td><td>Great</td></tr><tr><td>Interesting</td><td></td><td></td><td></td><td></td><td></td><td></td><td>Uninteresting</td></tr></table> Scoring: Exiting – 7 6 5 4 3 2 1 – Dull　Boring – 1 2 3 4 5 6 7 – Fun
End-of-unit tasks	Balance:　　　　　　　　　　　　Pre　　　Post　　% Change 1. Stand on line; one foot;　　　___ sec.　___ sec.　___ 　 eyes open; hands on hips 2. Stand on line; one foot;　　　___ sec.　___ sec.　___ 　 hands on hips 3. Repeat #1; jump and　　　　 ___ sec.　___ sec.　___ 　 turn 180°; land on line; 　 hold momentarily
Commerical instruments	Bruininks-Oseretsky Test of Motor Proficiency (Bruininks, 1978); sports skills (Stand & Wilson, 1993)

REFERENCES

Batzle, J. (1992). *Portfolio assessment and evaluation: Developing and using portfolios in the classroom.* Cypress, CA: Creative Teaching Press, Inc.

Belanoff, P., & Dickson, M. (Eds.). (1991). *Portfolios: Process and product.* Portsmouth, NH: Boynton/Cook Publishers.

Bruininks, R.H. (1978). *Bruininks-Oseretsky test of motor proficiency.* Circle Pines, MN: American Guidance Service.

Chittenden, E. (1991). Authentic assessment, evaluation, and documentation of student performance. In V. Perrone (Ed.), *Expanding student assessment* (pp. 22–31). Alexandria, VA: Association for Supervision and Curriculum Development.

Clemmons, J., Laase, L., Cooper, D., Areglado, N., & Dill, M. (1993). *Portfolios in the classroom: A teacher's sourcebook.* New York: Scholastic Professional Books.

DeFina, A.A. (1992). *Portfolio assessment: Getting started.* New York: Scholastic Professional Books.

Franck, M., Graham, G., Lawson, H., Loughrey, T., Ritson, R., Sanborn, M., & Seefeldt, V. (1992). *Physical education outcomes.* Reston, VA: National Association for Sport and Physical Education.

Gilbert, J.C. (1993). *Portfolio resource guide: Creating and using portfolios in the classroom.* Ottawa, KS: The Writing Conference, Inc.

Graham, G., Castenada, R., Hopple, C., Manross, M., & Sanders, S. (1992). *Developmentally apropriate physical education practices for children.* Reston, VA: National Association for Sport and Physical Education, Council on Physical Education for Children.

Kohl, P.L. (1992). Sharing the power: Fact or fallacy? *Action in Teacher Education, 14*(3), 29–36.

Levine, D.U., & Ornstein, A. C. (1993). School effectiveness and national reform. *Journal of Teacher Education, 44*(5), 335–45.

Marmo, D. (1994, April). *"Sport" folios—On the road to outcome-based education.* Paper presented at the AAHPERD National Convention, Denver, CO.

Meadors, W., Weinberg, W., Satterfield, N., & Lund, J. (1994, April). *School reform—The Kentucky response.* Paper presented at the AAHPERD National Convention, Denver, CO.

Meisels, S.J. (1993). The work sampling system: An authentic performance assessment. *Principal, 72*(5), 5–7.

Meisels, S.J., Dichtelmiller, M., Dorfman, A., Jablon, J.A., & Marsden, D.B. (1993). *The work sampling system resource guide.* Ann Arbor, MI: Rebus Planning Associates.

Melograno, V. (1985). *Designing the physical education curriculum: A self-directed approach* (2nd ed.). Dubuque, IA: Kendall/Hunt Publishing Company.

Melograno, V.J. (in press). *Designing the physical education curriculum* (3rd ed.). Champaign, IL: Human Kinetics Publishers.

Mohnsen, B., & Thompson, C. (1994, April). *The use of technology in authentic assessment.* Paper presented at the AAHPERD National Convention, Denver, CO.

Murphy, S., & Smith, M. (1992). *Writing portfolios: A bridge from teaching to assessment.* Markham, Ontario, Canada: Pippin Publishing Limited.

National Commission on Excellence in Education. (1983). *A nation at risk: The imperative for education reform.* Washington, DC: U.S. Government Printing Office.

Paulson, F.L., Paulson, P.R., & Meyer, C.A. (1991). What makes a portfolio a portfolio? *Educational Leadership, 48*(5), 60–63.

Perrone, V. (Ed.). (1991). *Expanding student assessment.* Alexandria, VA: Association for Supervision and Curriculum Development.

Siedentop, D. (Ed.). (1994). *Sport education.* Champaign, IL: Human Kinetics Publishers.

Strand, B.N., & Wilson, R. (1993). *Assessing sport skills.* Champaign, IL: Human Kinetics Publishers.

Tierney, R.J., Carter M.A., & Desai, L.E. (1991). *Portfolio assessment in the reading-writing classroom.* Norwood, MA: Christopher-Gordon Publishers, Inc.

U.S. Department of Education. (1991). *America 2000: An education strategy.* Washington, DC: U.S. Department of Education.

Viechnicki, K.J., Barbour, N., Shaklee, B., Rohrer, J., & Ambrose, R. (1993). The impact of portfolio assessment on teacher classroom activities. *Journal of Teacher Education, 44*(5), 371–77.

Zessoules, R., & Gardner, H. (1991). Authentic assessment: Beyond the buzzword and into the classroom. In V. Perrone (Ed.), *Expanding student assessment* (pp. 47–71). Alexandria, VA: Association for Supervision and Curriculum Development.

Student-Led Portfolio Conferences

by F. Leon Paulson and Pearl R. Paulson

ortfolio assessment offers a unique opportunity for students to take an active role in their own learning and explaining what they have learned to others. Portfolios support the concept that students should become independent, self-directed learners. Portfolio assessment is something students do, not something done to them. It is assessment that they can share with other people.

The concept of the portfolio comes from the arts. Artists produce collections of materials that tells a coherent story about themselves as artists. It is a way for them to demonstrate competence. Because no two artists are alike, no two portfolios are alike. But each portfolio gives a unique picture of individual skill and growth.

> **Portfolio assessment is something students do, not something done to them.**

One way to translate this traditional concept directly into the classroom is to encourage students to use their portfolios as part of a presentation they make about themselves as learners. Some schools are looking at replacing the traditional parent-teacher conference with student-led conferences. Rather than teachers and parents meeting to discuss the student's progress, the student becomes a participant, playing a central role in presenting him- or herself as a learner. As the name implies, the student takes charge of the conferences, using the portfolio much like artists use their portfolios. Student-led conferences have been used even at the kindergarten and primary levels.

Unpublished paper, August 1994. © 1994 by F. Leon Paulson and Pearl R. Paulson. Reprinted with permission.

But to use student-led conferences effectively, the students must be able to tell a story about themselves as learners. This requires that the students make decisions about their own portfolios. The students must be able to make good selections for the portfolio, and in order to make good selections, the students must be able to evaluate their work. Thus, the portfolio becomes more than the device that helps tell the story, it becomes part of the process through which the students learn to tell the story of their own learning. The portfolio become an integral part of the learning that is to be presented (see Paulson, Paulson, & Frazier, in press; and Paulson and Paulson, in press, for a discussion on how students can be encouraged to become more effective evaluators of their portfolios).

The idea of student-led conferences employing portfolios is catching on. In at least one school system, student-led conferences have begun to replace traditional report cards. When well done, parents come away with a feeling that they have learned more about their child's learning and progress than through a traditional report card. But there is an important additional benefit. Students can rise to the occasion and take charge of their own learning in important ways. When students are truly accountable for their own learning, they become more motivated to improve that learning.

Using student-led conferences effectively requires teachers to rethink some of their traditional roles. Teachers must develop new ways to interact with students and parents.

• For students to effectively present themselves as learners, they must learn to evaluate themselves. The focus of evaluation moves from teachers evaluating students to teachers teaching students to evaluate themselves. The teacher's role in evaluation changes.

• Students must take the lead in student-led conferences, not be put in the role of an audience member as the teacher talks about how well or poorly they are doing. The student is the presenter, the parents are the audience. Although teachers play an important and active role in helping students get ready for student-led conferences, they remain in the background as much as possible during the actual conference.

• If student-led conferences are to be effective, teachers must prepare students, parents, and possibly even school administrators. Some parents and administrators may be uneasy with an approach that has the student performing a task that is traditionally the teacher's. The teacher must make it clear that he or she plays a critically important role in student-led conferences, but that role is in helping students prepare themselves to conduct the conference in a competent manner.

Generally, parents respond positively to the student-led conferences.

• Finally, student-led conferences are innovative, and some parents may be uncomfortable with giving up the familiarity of traditional reporting formats like report cards. We recommend either continuing to use traditional reporting procedures along with student-led conferences, or, if you wish to change over, do so gradually.

Generally, parents respond positively to the student-led conferences, and most are satisfied that they have learned more about their child's learning than from traditional grades. Nevertheless, some parents may be concerned about how their child is performing as compared to other students, something student-led conferences are not designed to reveal. There are two things to consider when dealing with this kind of concern. First, be ready to hold a traditional parent-teacher conference during which you can address the student's learning from your perspective as teacher. Second, remember that traditional grading practices are highly variable from one classroom to another, one teacher to another. Therefore, it is difficult to argue that traditional grading practices give a realistic picture of how a child ranks with respect to other students.

Another parent concern might surface if students are "overrehearsed"—that is, they give what appears to be a rote, canned representation. In preparing for student-led conferences, create an atmosphere that supports conversation between student and parent.

PREPARING FOR STUDENT-LED CONFERENCES

A successful student-led conference is the culmination of careful planning and preparation. During the months leading up to the conference, the teacher must create an environment that is supportive and help students prepare themselves to take on what may be an unfamiliar role.

Preliminary Activities

How teachers introduce the concept and prepare the students is a key to successful conferences. Here is a list of things that should occur early in the school year.

1. Be sure everyone knows about the student-led conferences and is aware of the rationale for using them. As soon as possible, inform all involved that you will be holding student-led conferences and why. These groups include (but may not be limited to):

- The students,
- The parents,
- The principal,
- Other teachers in your building,
- District administration if the effort is widespread (in which case, hold a meeting for all teachers).

2. It is especially important to contact parents early. Here are some of the points that teachers should communicate, either in an open house for parents at the beginning of the year or by letter (see Anthony, et al., 1991).

- We are starting a new format for parent-teacher conferences. (It is usually best to emphasize that student-led conferences expand the conferences rather than eliminate a format many parents value.)
- You will receive a personal invitation from your child to attend a conference primarily with your youngster.
- These are the Goals for the conference.
  - accepting responsibility for their work,
  - learning to organize, present, and communicate,
  - learning to self-evaluate, and
  - becoming more acccountable.
- This is an opportunity for parents to show a positive interest in their child's progress and growth.
- The teacher will be in the room and available.
- You will be given the opportunity to meet privately with the teacher for a traditional parent-teacher meeting if you request.

• Remind parents to bring their child with them to the student-led conference. (Yes! We attended a student-led conference evening at one school in which the teachers had described the conferences at parent night, the children had written their parents invitations describing the conferences they would be leading, yet two separate sets of parents arrived for the student-led conferences without their student with them. We were at another student-led conference in which the parents brought their student with them but left the portfolio at home.)

Early Preparations

Once the school year has begun, there are several early steps that prepare the stage for successful student-led conferences. The first step in implementing student-led conferences is to build a communication link between parents and students. This should begin well in advance of the first student-led conference.

> **The first step in implementing student-led conferences is to build a communication link between parents and students.**

1. Talk about student-led conferences during the first parent night of the year, explain what it is about, and take questions.

2. Make it clear that any parent can request a parent-teacher conference after the student-led conference.

3. Develop a procedure that encourages students and their parents to respond to each other about the student's work. It is important to encourage the parents to respond to the student, not to you, the teacher.

> One technique is called "Two Stars and a Wish" (Hartmann, 1992, Appendix A). Each week or so, the student takes home a sheet of paper that tells two positive school experiences ("two stars") and one area in which the student is trying to improve ("and a wish"). Parents are asked to respond to the student in writing, being as positive as possible about the "stars" and as supportive as possible about the "wishes."

4. Some parents or administrators may fear that the student-led conference abdicates some of the teacher's responsibil-

ity. It is important that the purpose is carefully explained and the beneficial aspects of student involvement are clear (see "Goals" above). The communication link also gives you the opportunity to clearly establish that your role is changing from that of parent-teacher conference leader to that of teacher preparing students to assume more responsibility for their own learning.

Preparations Immediately Before the Conference

As the conference itself approaches, the pace of activities increases.

1. Students should begin preparing for the conference well in advance. Portfolio activities can support such preparations (see Hartmann, 1992). Hold brainstorming sessions with students regarding the kinds of things they would like to share. Have each student build a list of things they would like to share with parents. Remember, the student-led conference is an opportunity for the children to tell their own stories. Encourage each child to individually think through the challenge of understanding what they have learned and how to present that learning to their parents.

2. Work with the students in the weeks leading up to the conference. Discuss the kinds of things that make suitable entries and effective ways to display them. Treat the challenge as one of their presenting themselves and their learning in an accurate but positive light. Don't require them to put in anything they don't feel good about. Encourage students to write letters about their portfolios to be read by people looking at their portfolios.

3. A week or so ahead, have each child write a letter to the parents inviting them to the conference. Encourage the children to talk about the kinds of things the parents will see (Anthony, et al., 1992).

4. Encourage students to use the entire classroom as an environment to support their conferences. Students may take their parents to various learning stations of displays in the classroom to better explain their presentation.

5. It is a good idea to schedule one or more rehearsals. Some teachers start by holding model conferences in which the teacher plays the role of parent and another student leads the

discussion while the rest of the class watches. This is followed by having the students pair off and present their portfolios to each other (Hartmann, 1992). Some students do additional work on their portfolios following this experience.

THE CONFERENCE

There are many approaches to the conferences themselves. Conferences can be held one at a time similar to parent-teacher conferences, or for the entire class simultaneously. Some schools have conferences once a year, others quarterly. Choose whichever approach makes most sense with your students.

> **Put the students in charge of the conference as much as possible.**

1. Put the students in charge of the conference as much as possible. Let them help set up the interview schedule, arrange the room, arrange for parents to bring refreshments, and work out other details. It should be the students' show as much as possible. Beth Hebert, a principal whose elementary school holds portfolio evenings each spring, writes that the event "is really the children's evening, and they need to 'run the show' as much as possible. Parents and teachers have been impressed with the leadership and independence that even our youngest students have demonstrated in this setting" (Hebert, 1992, p. 61).

2. You, of course, must take the age of the student into account when using student-led conferences. Generally, younger children require more help and structuring while older children assume an increasingly independent role. Let us take a look at one way kindergarten teachers have found to support student-led conferences.

Teachers from the Touchstone Learning Center (a school serving grades K–3) in Lake Oswego, Oregon, developed a technique specifically to help kindergarten children run their own conferences. The teachers set up five "stations" in the classroom, each representing one part of the curriculum at the school. The five stations ensure that the young children will talk about curricula the teacher wants covered while reserving for the students as much choice as possible about what to put into their portfolios.

Portfolio. In the Touchstone program, students are given complete choice about what to place into their portfolios, thus children have a personal story to tell through their portfolios that may or may not focus on specific school curricula.

Writing. This station features the child's writing folder and copies of books they have published as part of the writing curriculum. The children particularly enjoy reading these books to the parents.

Physical Education. Touchstone includes a PE teacher who also does separate PE portfolios with the children. In these portfolios, the children learn to set fitness goals, track their own progress toward those goals, and work on drawings and other materials that allow them to find ways to relate the physical activities to concepts associated with muscles and the like.

Math. The math station emphasizes demonstration more than history of learning. The teacher has set out several math manipulations activities that the students can demonstrate as the parents watch.

Science. The science station includes several examples of hands-on science activities that the children are doing. For example, there may be small potted plants each child is growing.

Students and parents go through the conference in groups of five, each starting at one of the five stations. With fifteen children in the program, the teacher schedules 3 one-hour conferences. At each station, the children talk about and explain the activity and materials and answer parent's questions. After 8 minutes, the teacher's timer rings and the five groups rotate to the next station. Each station provides a structure that encourages each child to address specific parts of the curriculum; rotating stations guarantees that the discussion will be comprehensive. Prior to the conferences, the children had led practice conferences with their classmates.

The Touchstone teachers believe that this structure helps keep the conferences on-track with very little teacher intervention. In fact, the PE teacher initially planned to remain at the PE station but found that she felt like an intruder in a process that involved the students communicating with their parents about their progress. Touchstone feels that the added structure imposed by stations are unnecessary beyond the kindergarten level. Touchstone's first graders lead conferences from a single station.

Elmonica School in Beaverton, Oregon, also used centers for its first graders during the first conference in the fall. The staff posted charts describing the kinds of activities at each center to help parents know what is expected in case the children forgot.

3. Middle school offers challenges of its own. Students are reaching a stage where they can exercise considerable control not only leading their own conferences but in defining the situation itself to the visitors.

> Winnie Charley, a teacher at Jackson Middle School in Portland, Oregon, proposed to her students that they hold a portfolio evening during which they would invite parents to come to school and review their portfolios. The students felt particularly vulnerable at the prospect of sharing their work. They wanted to show parents what they were doing but they were concerned the atmosphere of the presentations remain positive.

> The class therefore designed, wrote, and produced (complete with recorded music) a series of brief skits which explained to parents exactly how they were supposed to act during the portfolio evening. Portfolio evening began with an audience of parents viewing the skits. "Arcenio Hall" interviewed famous people with opinions about portfolio evening, including Darth Vader who said, "Be nice to your child—I was nice to my child and its not easy for Darth Vader to be nice to anyone," and a brokenhearted Smurf who sobbed, "My parents put me down—don't put your child down." (For further information, see Appendix B to this paper.)

4. Unfortunately, not all parents are willing to attend such conferences, and some children do not have parents. It is important in such cases to find someone to fulfill the role of surrogate parent. Children living in institutions have caretakers who may be willing to help (Paulson & Paulson, 1992). It is important for the students to present their portfolios to a caring adult.

5. Occasionally some sort of prompting may be helpful, especially with younger children. Some teachers prepare sample questions that parents can ask their children. Such questions should focus on the child's presenting thoughtful explanations rather than rote recall (e.g., "Tell me about how you go about solving this problem" rather than "What is the answer?"). When stations are used (such as the Touchstone Kindergarten described above), it may be helpful to set up sample activities that the child can use to demonstrate skill and learning to the parents.

> **It is important that the teacher remain in the background as much as possible.**

MANAGEMENT CONCERNS

Here are some examples of things teachers have learned about managing student-led conferences. If there is a general rule-of-thumb, it is to allow the student to take as much responsibility for the event as possible.

The actual conferences are not difficult to manage. Students usually arrive accompanied by their parents. After introductions, the students and their parents can go directly to the place where the presentation will take place and begin. Be advised that younger siblings can be disruptive, especially if they are vying for attention. It may be wise to have an engaging activity prepared.

It is important that the teacher remain in the background as much as possible. Only occasionally should a teacher intervene, but then only to strengthen the child's presentation by redirecting the discussion or reminding the child of additional possibilities (Anthony, et al., 1991).

After the conference, the child may ask the parents to write a response. Be sure this portion remains positive. Parents should focus on progress, not dwell on shortcomings. It is useful for the teacher to have a class guest book for parents to sign and record comments. This should happen after the conference is completed so that you can get comments.

Conventional parent-teacher conferences last about 15 minutes, student-led conferences often last much longer. However, student-led conferences make it possible to hold more that one conference at a time. At several schools, all student-led conferences are held on a single day.

• Sandy Hartmann (1992), fifth grade teacher from Wyoming, Michigan, holds two conferences simultaneously in the same room. She circulates between the groups. She plans to double the length of each conference by holding four conferences simultaneously. Since conferences replace report cards in Sandy's class, she schedules student-led portfolios conferences four times a year.

• At Crow Island School (Hebert, 1992), there are as many as seven conferences going on simultaneously. Conferences are held in the spring.

• Both Touchstone Kindergarten (described above) and the first grade at Elmonica School in Beaverton held three to five conferences simultaneously, with parents rotating from station to station. Both found it disruptive when one of the parents arrived late. In both schools, all conferences are completed on a single date.

• At Cherry Park School in Portland's David Douglas district, three second grade teachers scheduled two sessions on a single night and divided their classes in half. Each session lasted about 1/2 hour (afterwards, one of the teachers said, "I felt more like a hostess than a teacher!"). The only problem was with the earlier group, in which some parents felt that the time was too short.

• The entire class led conferences simultaneously at Jackson Middle School (described above), making it possible for the evening to be introduced with a skit. All conferences lasted at least 45 minutes and several were still going strong after one hour.

After the conference, the teacher should give the class the opportunity to debrief and talk about the experience. This is also a good opportunity for them to think about changes they might want to make for next time.

OTHER ISSUES
Do not overlook the motivational impact of having students present their portfolios to people other than the parents. A visit

by the principal or an outsider who is interested in their work may stimulate considerable portfolio activity.

Students who assume responsibility for their own learning begin to set goals for themselves and monitor their own progress toward reaching those goals. Student-led conferences encourage this. Achieving this requires a supportive atmosphere where students are willing to present their work. Student-led conferences work in an atmosphere that is positive and supportive.

REFERENCES

Anthony, R. J., Johnson, T. D., Mickelson, N. I., & Preece, A. (1991). *Evaluating literacy: A perspective for change* (p. 161ff). Portsmouth, NH: Heinemann.

Hartmann, Sandy. (1992). Fifth grade teacher from Wyoming, Michigan. Video taped interview.

Hebert, E. A. (1992, May). Portfolios invite reflection—from students and staff. *Educational Leadership, 49*(8), 58–61.

Little, N., & Allan, J. (1988). *Student-led teacher parent conferences.* Toronto: Lugus Publications.

Paulson, F. L., & Paulson, P. R. (in press). The varieties of self-reflection. In Yancey, K. (Ed.). *Portfolios: Voices from the field.* Urbana, IL: National Council of Teachers of English.

Paulson, F. L., & Paulson, P. R. (1992, Summer). Afternoons to remember: Portfolio open houses for emotionally disabled students. *Portfolio News, 3*(4), 3, 7, 8–10.

Paulson, P. R., Paulson, F. L., & Frazier, D. M. (in press). Sarah's portfolio. In Yancey, K. (Ed.). *Portfolios: Voices from the field.* Urbana, IL: National Council of Teachers of English.

Appendix A
Two Stars and a Wish

Date: _____

Student Name: _____

Stars or compliments:
1.

2.

Wish or improvements:
1.

Parent:

Stars or compliments
1.

2.

Wish or improvement
1.

Source: Sandy Hartman, Wyoming, MI

Appendix B
Portfolio Evenings in a 7th Grade Class
Based on material supplied by Winifred Charley
Jackson Middle School, Portland

My interest in portfolios began about three years ago when I began teaching in middle school. My students began portfolios in the fall, but by January we usually lost steam. I just didn't follow through. I knew it was a good idea, but somehow I was falling short. I'd start again the next September, but somehow I never carried through all the way.

Then I heard and read about "portfolio evenings," in which students presented their portfolios to their parents. But the concept really frightened me. I could see a student sitting with his parents, showing them his portfolio and saying, "This is what I've learned this year," and the parents looking at the portfolio and saying, "Oh, my God, you haven't learned a thing. What kind of a ninny teaches you?" I wasn't ready to take the risk.

This year I became more serious when a portfolio class was offered by the district. During the course of the instruction, I saw some videos and read some articles about portfolio evenings that had succeeded in other parts of the country. So I tentatively suggested to my students that we might give a portfolio evening in the spring. When I mentioned the possibility to my principal, she loved it. Suddenly, I was giving a portfolio evening.

The Portfolio Program

My class is a seventh grade combination of writing, reading, and social studies. This year, the portfolios primarily reflected reading and writing although many students included examples of books they had read or reports they had written in social studies. Some of the things I had done earlier started to take on a more refined form this year. One of them was that after giving students a substantial writing assignment, I asked students to write a self-reflective statement before they handed it in for critique and assessment. I asked them to comment on several things, for example, the way they used verbs, whether their writing was more "alive," and the like. My intention was to get them thinking about the quality of their writing.

I also added a process through which I communicated directly with each student. I called it the Writing Goal Sheet. The Writing Goal

Sheet was a T-chart on which I listed things I noticed they did well and two or three suggestions for improvement. These became goals. Students wrote those on the Goal Sheet and the next time a writing assignment was due, they wrote a specific message explaining what they did to meet their goals. I returned that assignment with new goals, and so there was better follow through on goals.

In the area of reading, I introduced a record keeping procedure I call a "block assignment" which allowed students to keep track of their reading. It dealt with areas like content, attitude, or striving for excellence. Their grade was tied to how many blocks they completed. Every Friday they analyzed their reading and filled in the blocks.

Also, early in the year, I asked students to write me a message telling me about themselves, describing themselves as a writer and a learner. That was one of their first self-reflective activities. We did this again at progress report time and at other times throughout the year.

We divided the portfolios into several sections.

• The first section was for reading. This included the block assignments, reading journals, and a list describing themselves as readers.

• The second section was for writing. They included their list describing themselves as a writer followed by material from the full process writing program that I asked them to put into their portfolios. The section also included their Goal Sheet listing the areas in writing each was working on. In addition, I asked them to include a major research report assignment that they had done at the end of the first semester.

• The third section included their selection of work according to criteria I specified. From their writing folders I asked them to pull an example of their "best work" and attach an explanation of why they thought it was their best work. I also asked them to choose an example of something they really liked and to write a short paragraph about why they liked it. Finally, I asked them to chose something they had struggled with and to add a note explaining why it was such a struggle.

• The fourth section of the portfolio was the self-reflection section. Here they wrote about how they felt they were doing in reading, writing, social studies, and as a cooperative group member midpoint in the quarter, at the end of the quarter, and at other key times. I also asked them to keep a process diary during their big research project. The diary tracked how their understanding changed as they went along.

• The final section of the portfolio was compliments. If someone in my class really helps another student understand something, that student writes a compliment saying, for example, "Pat really helped me understand what the main idea is." The student would sign and date it and give it to Pat. Ultimately, it would show up in the compliment section of Pat's portfolio.

Preparing the Portfolios

Active preparations for portfolio evening began about six weeks before the date was set. We began with group brainstorming sessions in which I encouraged the students to recall what they had learned this year in reading and writing.

After the brainstorming sessions on what they had learned collectively, I asked each student to make a list of how he or she had changed as a reader or a writer during their seventh grade year. Once they had made their claims on paper, I asked them to go into their work and find evidence to support the claims. They attached "Post-Its" to places in their portfolios that demonstrated an example of their growth. For example, if a student claimed to understand what a theme was, he or she would attach a Post-It in his or her reading journal or piece of writing that indicated that this illustrated an example of their understanding of the theme.

Preparations for Portfolio Evening

As portfolio evening approached, I tried to involve student as much as possible. We set up four committees. One was in charge of making the classroom look good. A second was in charge of hospitality such as calling parents and arranging refreshments. The third thought through the space requirements. And the fourth planned a skit that would explain to parents what to expect during the course of the portfolio evening. The committees were a good idea because every student in the class was involved. It meant that, along with presenting their portfolios, each had an additional reason for being there that night. The committees helped generate enthusiasm for portfolio evening.

Three weeks before the evening took place, we sent a letter home to parents describing portfolio evening and asking them to reserve the date. The hospitality committee came up with a very nice invitation and a request for an RSVP, which we sent out three days before the portfolio evening. The kids also decided on the refreshments they would like (cupcakes and 7-Up) and made a list of parents who they thought would bring refreshments and called the parents. Really, they did it all themselves!

The setup committee had a really good idea that was different from mine and their idea turned out to be the best idea. They decided to use the large area central to all 7th grade classrooms for the common meeting place. They moved some desks from the classroom into this area so that desks could be spaced far apart for privacy. We also borrowed other teachers' classrooms so that there were no more than six student conferences in any one room.

The Portfolio Evening

As they entered, the visitors were greeted by a small theater style setting with all chairs facing the front of the central area. The portfolios were lined up (in alphabetical order) on a table at right and the hospitality table was close by. Clearly, everything was ready for an event when the portfolio skit began at 7:15.

The skit, written, directed, and produced by the students, was in an entertainment talk show format ("The Arcenio Hall Show") in which the emcee interviewed various fictional and real characters (e.g., Darth Vader, a Smurf, their teacher). The skit, though entertaining, had a serious message—it told the parents to look at learning as something that was in progress and not to expect perfect, finished work. The class was in the process of learning and the parents would see things wrong (spelling, punctuation), but they would see growth and learning. The point was to celebrate accomplishments, not criticize shortcomings. The skit was entertaining and got the evening rolling in a lighthearted way.

After the skit, the students got their portfolios and escorted their parents to one of the conference centers. Students simply went through their portfolios and talked about what they had learned during the year, often documenting their accomplishments by showing examples identified by the Post-Its. The evening was low key but intense. The skit had put the parents into the right mindset. Nobody was critical. Everyone was very accepting and in just about every case they saw growth.

There were some instances I really did worry about—students whose portfolios were kind of thin and the students hadn't tried very hard that year. This was where I was afraid I was going to be "fined" because I didn't do a good enough job teaching the student. It really didn't turn out that way. I'm thinking of one family, new to the district, who had complained at a PTA meeting that our West Coast schools weren't up to par with East Coast schools. When I checked my records, I found that their student hadn't been turning in any homework. The conference itself was one of the few cases where there was tension between the parents and the student. The portfolio told a clear story of a student who had done little during the semester (in fact, I had privately noticed the mother sneaking a peek at other student's portfolios earlier in the evening). During the portfolio evening the father sought me out and commented that the portfolio spoke for itself and it was evident that his son hadn't been working very hard all year. I was relieved not to be blamed.

Reflections

I was very pleased with how portfolio evening turned out and would recommend it. But, portfolio evenings take a lot of energy—they do not happen by themselves. It takes a lot of classroom time to do it right. It takes support from the administration to keep the school building open in the evening. It takes support from parents and energy from the teacher because your enthusiasm goes over to the kids.

We set no time limit and the students and the parents conferred for close to an hour. I used a response form in which I asked parents to give their child two compliments and state one area where they would like to see improvement ("Two Stars and a Wish"). Comments on this form were warm and supportive. Parents really appreciated the opportunity to talk.

One boy in my class is from a broken home. At the conclusion of the evening, his father told me that he really enjoyed it because for seven years he asked his son how things at school were going and the boy answered "OK." "Tonight, my son told me how school was. Tonight, I really found out what was going on." His son commented, "I like portfolio evening much better than parent-teacher conferences because parents and teachers talk about you when you're sitting there and you feel very unimportant. Tonight I felt like I was important. I had something to say."

Portfolios and Your Child: Some Questions and Answers for Parents and Families

by the Vermont State Department of Education

W HAT IS A PORTFOLIO?
It is a collection of a student's work, one that holds schoolwork specially chosen to show what the student can do.

Usually a portfolio is different from a work folder, which might hold *all* of a student's current pieces or projects. The portfolio contains the student's *best efforts*—and it gives the student a chance to reflect on the quality and development of his/her work. Vermont schools use portfolios to help develop students' writing and their problem-solving skills in mathematics.

WHY USE PORTFOLIOS?
There are a number of good reasons. Here are a few:

• Portfolios allow us to look at several examples of student work—at a *range* of writing or problem-solving skills.

• Because the drafts of students' work are usually included, portfolios let us see how final products were developed.

• Portfolios give students, teachers, and parents a way to look at how well a student's work compares with established standards for good writing or mathematics.

• They also give us a way to look at students' growth and development over time.

A booklet developed by the Vermont State Department of Education, 1994. © 1994 by the Vermont State Department of Education, Montpelier, VT 05620. Reprinted with permission.

• At the 4th and 8th grade levels, Vermont students' portfolios are evaluated as part of the statewide student assessment program—to see how well students meet the standards of good writing and mathematics.

Standards are the goals we set for high-level student performance. Our Vermont standards make it clear, across the state, what the critical building blocks of good writing and problem-solving are.

The purpose of the state's assessment program is *not* to rank or sort individual students. It is to find out how well our students write and solve problems, and to help them improve their skills.

HOW DO PORTFOLIOS DIFFER FROM TRADITIONAL WAYS OF LOOKING AT STUDENTS' WRITING AND MATH SKILLS?

• Unlike a simple report-card grade of A–, C, or S+, portfolios give us a way to see *actual student performance,* and to evaluate how much the student's projects show the features of good writing and mathematics.

• Unlike single tests, portfolios show real writing and problem-solving, using students' daily work—and they allow the students to choose, with teacher guidance, what goes into the portfolio.

• Unlike a simple folder of student work, portfolios help us compare student work to standards that are clear and are shared with students, parents, and others.

WHAT GOES INTO A PORTFOLIO?

In *writing,* required pieces for a portfolio that will be assessed include:

• an imaginative piece: a poem, short story, or play.

• a personal response—perhaps to a book, current event, sports event, or personal experience.

• writing from a subject other than language arts (in 4th grade, one piece of writing; in 8th grade, three pieces).

• a "best piece" of writing, selected by the student, sometimes with help from the teacher.

- a letter, by the student, about the best piece or portfolio.
- a table of contents.

In *mathematics*, the portfolio should include:
- seven "best practices" that show good problem-solving, and show students' best work in each of the criteria. (Good problems can usually be solved in more than one way and might have more than one right answer.)
  - 10 to 15 other pieces.
  - a letter to the evaluator.

WHO CHOOSES WHAT GOES IN?
The student decides, with the teacher's help, what goes into the portfolio. Often the contents of the portfolio change as the year goes on, and as students develop better and better work.

HOW IS A PORTFOLIO EVALUATED?
Writing portfolios are evaluated in five ways:
1. Is the *purpose* of the writing clear?
2. How *well organized* is the writing?
3. Do the *details* help the writing?
4. Does the writing have *"voice"* or appropriate tone?
5. Does the writing show acceptable *grammar, usage*, and *mechanics?*

Each of these questions is answered with one of the following responses:
- "extensively"
- "sometimes"
- "frequently"
- "rarely"

So, for example, a piece of writing might be assessed as having "frequently" used rich details, but only "rarely" showing acceptable grammar, usage, and mechanics.

Mathematics portfolios are evaluated by looking at students' pieces for evidence of two types of skills: problem-solving and communication.

Problem-solving skills:
1. How well does the student *understand* the task?
2. What *strategy* does the student use to solve the problem?
3. What *kinds of decisions* does the student make?
4. Is the student able to *extend the solution?* (That is, can the student make observations about the solution, make connections to the real problem, and develop a rule or formula for similar problems?)

Math communication skills:
1. How well does the student use *math language*— vocabulary, symbols, and notation?
2. Does the student use *graphs, tables, charts, diagrams,* or *models?*
3. How *clearly* does the student present his/her work?

Each question is answered with one of the following ratings:

Level 4: Work shows "sophistication"
Level 3: Work shows "proficiency"
Level 2: "Novice or beginner" work
Level 1: Little or no evidence to meet the criterion was found

HOW ARE THE RESULTS OF PORTFOLIO ASSESSMENT USED?

• *Students* use portfolio results to focus their efforts on areas that need improvement. Usually, students' work shows strength in some areas and needs in others. In most classes, students continually use the program's standards to look at and improve their own work.

In writing, for example, a student may review a piece with a friend, compare it to sample "benchmark" pieces, and find that his own work is well-organized but lacks detail. The student may then revise the writing to add rich, well-chosen details.

In math, a student may compare her work with a benchmark example and see that she needs to make better use of math language. She then has some insight, and a useful model, to help her improve her work in this way.

• *Teachers* use portfolio results to help them fit their instruction to their students' needs. Teachers periodically assess student work to help them adjust what and how they are teaching—often for individual students, but sometimes for the class or writing/ math program as a whole. Finally, toward the end of the year, teachers review and score students' whole portfolios.

> *Teachers* **use portfolio results to help them fit their instruction to their students' needs.**

Teachers often use portfolio information as part of what they report to parents at conference or report-card time. Portfolio results do not translate directly into grades, but they help to communicate student progress.

Portfolios are usually passed on from year to year, building into a collection that reflects a student's whole academic career. (In most cases, only some of the pieces are passed along; the rest go home.) This information is helpful to the student's next teacher, and often the student will continue to work on a project from the previous year.

• *Administrators and school board members* use portfolio results to help build a "big picture" of how well students are learning. They use the information to celebrate the strong areas of the school or district, and to identify needs for additional resources or staff development.

• *The state of Vermont* uses portfolio results to provide some of the data for a statewide picture of how well Vermont students write and solve problems in mathematics. Also, several students' portfolios are randomly selected from each school or district for review by a statewide group of teachers—to help identify areas of strength and areas that need assistance.

• *Parents* can use portfolio results to see how their children's learning and skills grow over time, to see the range of youngsters' writing and math work, and to see how much the work shows the features of good writing and mathematics.

HOW CAN I KNOW IF MY CHILD IS PROGRESSING?
There are several ways to think about student progress in writing and mathematics:

- First of all, look for *growth over time.* Try to save samples of student work from year to year—and even within a year, from September to January to May. Be sure to talk about what you see!

- Ask the teacher what kinds of *goals* he/she has set for (and with) your youngster. Ask how you can observe progress toward these goals.

- You might also want to take a look at some of the *sample* or *benchmark pieces,* which illustrate the range of student work at different grade levels. You might ask about these at a parent conference.

- Finally, consider some basic questions:

> Can my child talk more now about what makes good writing and problem solving?
> Does he/she seem to enjoy writing and problem solving?
> Is my youngster writing more often? Writing *more?*
> Is he/she solving problems with different approaches, and using more math language?
> Is he/she proud of what is written, and of the problem he/she has solved?

WHAT IF MY CHILD HAS SPECIAL NEEDS? SHOULDN'T HE/SHE HAVE A PORTFOLIO TOO?
Absolutely. Everyone who can communicate in some way or other should have a portfolio.

Some students with special needs who have an IEP (Individualized Educational Plan) may have some accommodations specified for their particular disability or condition. For example, some students may need computers with large print or special assistance in organizing their work. But *everyone* can develop writing and problem-solving skills, and can benefit from clear standards and frequent writing/problem-solving experiences. Special needs students usually respond very well when they are presented with the same opportunities and clear expectations as their classmates.

WHAT CAN PARENTS AND FAMILY MEMBERS DO TO HELP?

- *Show interest* in the student's writing and problem solving. Ask what kinds of things are going into the portfolio, and what the student thinks he/she does best as a writer or problem solver.

- *When you visit* school, ask to see the student's portfolio. If possible, have the student explain to you what's in it, and why.

- *When you talk to the teacher*—by phone, in parent conferences, or just visiting—talk about students' writing and math. What do you notice about the writing or problem solving? What does the teacher notice?

- *When you read aloud*—from the newspaper, a magazine, or a book—sometimes stop to comment on what you notice about the author's style or strategies.

- *When you use mathematics* to solve problems, or see someone else thinking through a problem (for example, estimating the cost of a trip or the length of time it will take to get there), comment on what strategies are used. (Charting? Drawing a picture?) *Talk* about how the problem was solved, and what you think about the answer.

- *Try to increase the amount of out-of-school writing and mathematics* that students do—not by adding homework, but by using writing and problem solving on an everyday basis.

Here are some possibilities:
Writing: Lists, reminder notes to family members, poems, letters, awards, letters to the editor, complaints, journals, etc.!

Mathematics: Charts, puzzles, doubling or reducing recipes, estimating costs, distances, time, space, materials, etc.!

"Modeling" writing and problem solving yourself really helps. *You don't need to be an expert or a teacher.* Just write, solve problems, and notice your youngster's progress. Those are among the most important things you can do.

Portfolios Invite Reflection—from Students *and* Staff

by Elizabeth A. Hebert

Four years ago, Crow Island Elementary School began a project that has reaped benefits far beyond what any of us could have imagined. The focus of the project was assessment of children's learning, and the tangible product is a new reporting form augmented by student portfolios.

More important, however, has been the process of developing our thinking and teaching around new ways of looking at children's learning. In fact, this process became more valuable to us as a faculty than the assessment product, helpful as it has been.

> The project grew out of our dissatisfaction and frustration with mandated standardized modes of assessment.

OUR COMMITMENT TO ALTERNATIVE ASSESSMENT

The project grew out of our dissatisfaction and frustration with mandated standardized modes of assessment. Standardized tests do not reflect how we teach, the effects of our teaching on children, or how we adapt instruction to individual learners. Wolf and colleagues write that "the design and implementation of alternative modes of assessment will entail nothing less than a wholesale transition from what we call a *testing* culture to an *assessment* culture." They continue:

From *Educational Leadership*, vol. 49, no. 8, May 1992, pp. 58–61. © 1992 by the Association for Supervision and Curriculum Development. Reprinted with permission.

The observable differences in the form, the data, and the conduct of standardized testing and its alternatives are in no way superficial matters or mere surface features. They derive from radical differences in underlying conceptions of mind and of the evaluation process itself. Until we understand these differences and their network of consequences, we cannot develop new tools that will allow us to ensure that a wide range of students use their minds well. (1991, p. 33)

Obviously, we had our work cut out for us. What did we do to reaffirm our commitment to a concept of learning incompatible with standardized testing? First, we did a good deal of reading; engaged in lengthy discussions about values, community building, and conferencing; and consulted with experts. We also became more deliberate about making time to visit one another's classrooms and to share and refine our observations of children. Next we began defining the questions to which we were seeking answers. Our first questions were global:

- How do we define learning?
- Where does learning take place?
- How do we recognize learning?
- How do we report instances of learning?

As we answered these larger questions, our concerns became more specific. How can we communicate about children's learning experiences with parents in ways that:

- authentically describe the child,
- speak to issues of accountability and maintain the integrity of our beliefs about children and how they learn,
- reflect the different ways that teachers organize instruction,
- provide concrete information compatible with parents' expectations?

A COMPATIBLE THEORY

Some background information about our school provides a context for our project and how we went about answering these questions. Crow Island is a public JK–5 school in Winnetka, Illinois, an affluent suburb of Chicago's north shore. The

Winnetka Public Schools include three elementary schools and one middle school for grades 6–8. Our lower schools have enrollments of 360–390. Although a public school system, we have a strong tradition in the progressive philosophy of education that is distinguished by:

> **Gardner's theory provided a good scaffold for our thinking.**

- a commitment to a developmental orientation to instruction,
- the priority placed on consideration of the "whole child" and his or her individual model of learning,
- the absence of letter grades until 7th grade,
- high regard for teachers as professionals.

In acknowledging the uniqueness of a child's mode of learning, the district has placed a high priority on conferencing with parents. For many years, pupil progress has been reported to parents in a conference format three times per year. Teachers had prepared narrative descriptions of children using the following organizers: language arts, math, social studies, science, growth of the child as a group member.

One expert who influenced our thinking about alternative assessment was Howard Gardner, whose "Theory of Multiple Intelligences" (musical, linguistic, logical-mathematical, spatial, bodily-kinesthetic, interpersonal, and intrapersonal) challenges the more traditional concepts of intelligence. The main thrust of Gardner's theory as applied to schools is that children may demonstrate the different kinds of intelligences in ways not necessarily associated with traditional school subjects and certainly not associated with traditional modes of assessment. Gardner's theory resonated with the themes of progressive education to which we at Crow Island are devoted.

A VISUAL FORMAT

Gardner's theory provided a good scaffold for our thinking. The next step was to put our thoughts into a visual format. Our first rough attempt began to capture the idea of multiple dimensions of a child's learning. This primitive model consisted of a stick figure surrounded by floating boxes. As you may expect, there

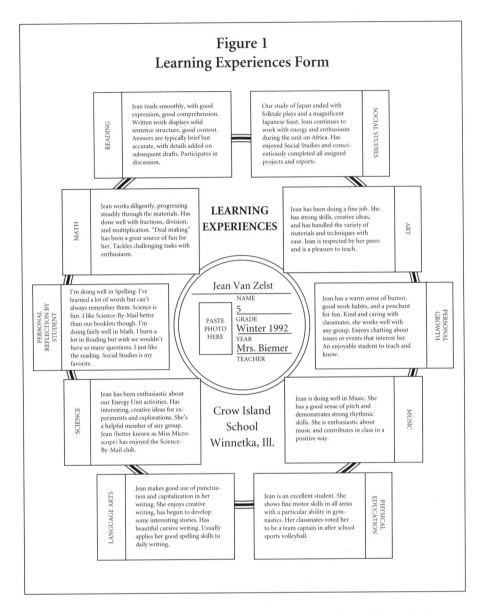

Figure 1
Learning Experiences Form

READING
Jean reads smoothly, with good expression, good comprehension. Written work displays solid sentence structure, good content. Answers are typically brief but accurate, with details added on subsequent drafts. Participates in discussion.

SOCIAL STUDIES
Our study of Japan ended with folktale plays and a magnificent Japanese feast. Jean continues to work with energy and enthusiasm during the unit on Africa. Has enjoyed Social Studies and conscientiously completed all assigned projects and reports.

LEARNING EXPERIENCES

MATH
Jean works diligently, progressing steadily through the materials. Has done well with fractions, division, and multiplication. "Deal making" has been a great source of fun for her. Tackles challenging tasks with enthusiasm.

ART
Jean has been doing a fine job. She has strong skills, creative ideas, and has handled the variety of materials and techniques with ease. Jean is respected by her peers and is a pleasure to teach.

PERSONAL REFLECTION BY STUDENT
I'm doing well in Spelling. I've learned a lot of words but can't always remember them. Science is fun. I like Science-By-Mail better than our booklets though. I'm doing fairly well in Math. I learn a lot in Reading but wish we wouldn't have so many questions. I just like the reading. Social Studies is my favorite.

Jean Van Zelst
NAME
5
GRADE
Winter 1992
YEAR
Mrs. Biemer
TEACHER
PASTE PHOTO HERE

PERSONAL GROWTH
Jean has a warm sense of humor, good work habits, and a penchant for fun. Kind and caring with classmates, she works well with any group. Enjoys chatting about issues or events that interest her. An enjoyable student to teach and know.

SCIENCE
Jean has been enthusiastic about our Energy Unit activities. Has interesting, creative ideas for experiments and explorations. She's a helpful member of any group. Jean (better known as Miss Microscope) has enjoyed the Science-By-Mail club.

Crow Island School
Winnetka, Ill.

MUSIC
Jean is doing well in Music. She has a good sense of pitch and demonstrates strong rhythmic skills. She is enthusiastic about music and contributes in class in a positive way.

LANGUAGE ARTS
Jean makes good use of punctuation and capitalization in her writing. She enjoys creative writing, has begun to develop some interesting stories. Has beautiful cursive writing. Usually applies her good spelling skills to daily writing.

PHYSICAL EDUCATION
Jean is an excellent student. She shows fine motor skills in all areas with a particular ability in gymnastics. Her classmates voted her to be a team captain in after school sports volleyball.

was much discussion about the number, size, and positioning of the boxes, but we finally agreed on a format. We call it our Learning Experiences Form (see fig. 1 for a composite example of the form, shortened for space).

Our next concern was to identify our organizers on the Learning Experiences Form. Being committed to the multiple intelligences perspective, we readily included music, art, and physical education. We wanted to recognize these teachers' long-term relationships with students, the value of their programs, and their insights about children's learning. But what about the other Learning Experience organizers? The dialogue went something like this:

Q: How should I specify my organizers?
A: That depends on how you organize instruction.
Q: But what if mine are different from someone else's?
A: That's OK. You organize instruction differently. We already know that about one another. Now we're just writing about it.
Q: But we organize instruction differently for different students.
A: Your Learning Experiences Form will then reflect the flexibility of your teaching.

This was a crucial stage in our thinking because discussing the form brought to the surface what I term the "bilingualism" of teachers. *Inside language*—what we do in our classrooms—reflects our beliefs and values, years of teaching experience, observations of children and of other good teachers, and confidence in knowing what we know. *Outside language*—what we say we do in our classrooms—is influenced by community values, comfort level within the school environment, political pressures, district and administrative policies, test scores, and curriculum.

The nature of our project necessitated our speaking "inside language," a more difficult discourse because it requires feelings of safety and security. Gradually, though, we were able to experience the sharing of values that leads to the creation of a secure, thoughtful environment for children, teachers, and parents.

A CLOSE LOOK AT OURSELVES

In order to change how we evaluated children's learning, we realized we needed to take a close look at ourselves. We soon found ourselves undergoing an intensive assessment of our teaching, our beliefs about children, and our views of the school and its relationship to our community.

At this point, the project quite naturally proceeded from an emphasis on student assessment to a more powerful staff development focus. In order for this to occur in any school, administrators must commit to providing the kind of school environment where such a climate can flourish. Administrators also have to acknowledge that all teachers do not arrive at the same point in their growth together. As we emphasize with the children, teachers must construct their own knowledge of children, how they learn, and how to evaluate that learning. We have to be patient and sufficiently open to allow for different stages of understanding, yet focused enough to provide clarity and vision to the effort.

> Teachers must construct their own knowledge of children, how they learn, and how to evaluate that learning.

IMPROVEMENT TO THE PROCESS

We began using the Learning Experiences Form in a variety of ways. Some teachers were more conservative, using traditional school subject labels on their forms. Other coined new organizers that reflected their teaching styles. As they struggled with the new format, teachers became more thoughtful; and parents, sensing the positive energy and concern of teachers, responded enthusiastically. After the first conference using the new form, the response from both parents and teachers was overwhelmingly positive.

Over four years, we've refined the form to meet the suggestions of teachers at kindergarten, primary, and intermediate levels. In response to our concern about how to separate out curriculum specifics and descriptions of a child's learning, one of our teachers designed a Curriculum Overview, to be printed on the back of the form, that consists of mini-statements of curriculum objectives for that portion of the year. This addition freed up the front of the form for more focused descriptions of children's learning.

Noting the absence of the child's input to the form, we designated a space for a "child's reflection" about his or her learning. The older students write their own thoughts; teachers take dictation for the 1st graders. We've also begun to include parents' thoughts about their child's learning experience in our assessment form.

STUDENTS TELL THEIR STORIES

The next step was to have our students create portfolios. Portfolios are compatible with Crow Island's agenda for effective teaching, authentic assessment, and faculty growth. One of the best definitions in the current literature comes from Paulson and Paulson (1991): "Portfolios tell a story . . . put in anything that helps tell the story." With these authors, we also agree about the importance of the child's participation in selecting the contents of the portfolio and with a focus more on process than on content (1991, p. 1).

> **At present, each of our students has a portfolio that represents work across all domains.**

At present, each of our students has a portfolio that represents work across all domains. Students maintain their portfolios all year and frequently have conferences with the teacher about works in progress, additions, and deletions. At the end of the year, their portfolios are combined with past years' work and stored in our Student Archives. The archives are alphabetically arranged in open shelving in our Resource Center along with historical documents, publications, and photographs of our school and students.

PORTFOLIO EVENINGS

Three years ago we added a new element to our assessment project. Encouraged by the kinds of thinking that children have expressed in their Student Reflections, we realized that they were capable of much more. Getting them more involved in the process of assessment seemed to make good sense.

In preparation for "Portfolio Evenings," children review their portfolio/archive as teachers guide them with questions like:

• How has your writing changed since last year (or since September)?

- What do you know about numbers now that you didn't know in September?
- Let's compare a page from a book you were reading last year and a book you are reading now and include copies of each in your portfolio (an idea from Denise Levine, Fordham University, New York).
- What is unique about your portfolio?
- What would you like Mom and Dad to understand about your portfolio? Can you organize it so it will show that?

The idea is to ask guiding questions that help children reflect on their learning. Students are encouraged to write about their learning and to include these thoughts as part of their portfolios. Developing the metacognitive process in students, even at a young age, heightens their awareness and commitment to a critical assessment of their learning.

> **Students are encouraged to write about their learning and to include these thoughts as part of their portfolios.**

In preparation for Portfolio Evenings, the teacher divides the class into small groups of six or seven at the primary level (and larger groups at grades 4 and 5) and assigns a night for each group of students and their parents. Primary-level Portfolio Evenings are held in February. We hold intermediate-level Portfolio Evenings in May, because older students prepare more extensive projects.

On Portfolio Evenings, which last for about an hour and a half, the children sit with their parents and present their portfolios. The teacher and I circulate, visiting each student and highlighting particular milestones each youngster may have attained. We are available for questions but try not to intrude, because this is really the children's evening, and they need to "run the show" as much as possible. Parents and teachers have been impressed with the leadership and independence that even our youngest students have demonstrated in this setting.

A POWERFUL LEARNING EXPERIENCE

We are continuing to refine our assessment project. Some issues we're addressing are practical in nature, for example, storage containers for the portfolios/archives. Others are more fundamental, like how to use portfolios to link children's early, strong expressions of interest in a particular topic to more sophisticated elaborations later in their school careers. We are also contemplating how to gain the community's support for these alternative modes of assessment as part of a viable system of accountability. And, finally, as a faculty we are trying to preserve the cohesive and bold spirit that nurtured this project along its way.

The entire process has been a powerful learning experience for our faculty as well as for the children and their parents. It has expressed the fundamental values of our school district and represents our joint exploration of the complex issues of children and their learning. We are encouraged to go forward by the positive effects this project has had on the self-esteem and professionalism of the individual teachers and the inevitable strengthening of the professional atmosphere of the entire school. We have improved our ability to assess student learning. Equally important, we have become, together, a more empowered, effective faculty.

Author's note: For further reading on student archives, consult the writings of Pat Carini and teachers from the Prospect School in Bennington, Vermont, The Prospect Archive and Center for Education and Research, Bennington, VT 05257.

REFERENCES

Gardner, H. (1983). *Frames of Mind: The Theory of Multiple Intelligences.* New York: Basic Books.

Paulson, F. L., and P. R. Paulson. (Copyright, February 1991). "Portfolios: Stories of Knowing." Prepublication draft.

Paulson, F. L., P. R. Paulson, and C. Meyer. (1991). "What Makes a Portfolio a Portfolio?" *Educational Leadership* 48, 5: 60–63.

Wolf, D., J. Bixby, J. Glen, and H. Gardner. (1991). "To Use Their Minds Well: Investigating New Forms of Student Assessment." In *Review of Research in Education* 17, edited by G. Grant, p. 33. Washington, D.C.: American Educational Research Association.

Authors

Leslie Ballard has taught at the secondary and college levels for nineteen years. She currently teaches English at Terre Haute North High School and is a member of the editorial board of the *Journal of Teaching Writing.*

Helen C. Barrett is assistant professor and coordinator of educational technology at the University of Alaska, Anchorage School of Education.

Susan Belgrad is assistant professor of education at Roosevelt University, Chicago, Illinois. She coauthored *The Mindful School: The Portfolio Connection.*

Susan Black is a research columnist for *The Executive Educator,* a writer and educational consultant, and adjunct professor of graduate studies at Elmira College, New York, and the University of Maine.

Kay Burke is a former teacher, an author, and a national presenter of staff development workshops. She authored *The Mindful School: How to Assess Authentic Learning* and coauthored *The Mindful School: The Portfolio Connection.*

Linda Darling-Hammond is a professor at Teachers College, Columbia University, and co-director of the National Center for Restructuring Education, Schools, and Teaching. She authored *Authentic Assessment in Action: Studies of Schools and Students at Work.*

Brenda S. Engel is senior research associate in the School of Arts and Sciences, Lesley College, Cambridge, Massachusetts.

Louis M. Fisher III is the coordinator of research and development at Learning Quest, Inc., in Corvallis, Oregon, and designer and programmer of LabQuest and Learning Quest's electronic portfolio.

Robin Fogarty has trained teachers throughout the world in cognitive strategies and cooperative interaction. She has authored, coauthored, and edited numerous publications in the field, including *The Mindful School: The Portfolio Connection.*

Judith Fueyo is an assistant professor at The Pennsylvania State University. She teaches language arts, emergent literacy, composition, teacher research, and portfolio culture.

Susan Mandel Glazer is professor of graduate studies and director of the Center for Reading and Writing at Rider University in New Jersey. Susan has authored and coauthored thirteen books and more than one hundred articles.

Elizabeth A. Hebert, Ph.D., is principal of Crow Island School, Winnetka, Illinois. She has written about and lectured extensively on the subject of student portfolios.

Kristine Luberto is an elementary teacher in the West Windsor-Plainsboro school district in New Jersey. She is currently working on her master of arts degree at Rider University.

Vincent J. Melograno is a professor and associate dean at Cleveland State University and author of *Designing the Physical Education Curriculum.*

Carol A. Meyer is an evaluation specialist for Beaverton School District in Beaverton, Oregon.

Christopher Moersch is the director of the National Business Alliance in Corvallis, Oregon.

F. Leon Paulson is a specialist for the Multnomah County Education Service District. He has written widely on the use of portfolios in classroom instruction.

Pearl R. Paulson is director of special education for the Gladstone School District. She has written widely on the use of portfolios in classroom instruction.

Katrin-Kaja Rooman is an elementary teacher in the West Windsor-Plainsboro school district in New Jersey. She received her master of arts degree from Rider University.

Dennie Palmer Wolf is senior research associate at the Harvard Graduate School of Education and director of PACE (Performance Assessment Collaboratives for Education), a multiyear project in diversifying approaches to assessment.

Acknowledgments

Grateful acknowledgment is made to the following authors, publishers, and agents for their permission to reprint copyrighted materials.

SECTION 1
National Association of Secondary School Principals (NASSP) for "Setting Standards for Students: The Case for Authentic Assessment" by Linda Darling-Hammond. From *NASSP Bulletin,* vol. 77, no. 556, November 1993, p. 18–26. Reprinted with permission. All rights reserved. (For more information about NASSP services and/or programs, please call 703-860-0200.)

Kappa Delta Pi, an International Honor Sociaty in Education, for "Portfolio Assessment and the New Paradigm: New Instruments and New Places" by Brenda S. Engel. From *The Educational Forum,* vol. 59, no. 1, Fall 1994, p. 22–27. Reprinted with permission. All rights reserved.

F. Leon Paulson and Pearl R. Paulson for "Assessing Portfolios Using the Constructivist Paradigm" by F. Leon Paulson and Pearl R. Paulson. A paper presented at the Annual Meeting of the American Educational Research Association (New Orleans, Louisiana, April 4–8, 1994). Reprinted with permission. All rights reserved.

National School Boards Association for "Portfolio Assessment" by Susan Black. From *The Executive Educator,* vol. 15, no. 1, February 1993, pp. 28–31. Reprinted with permission. All rights reserved.

SECTION 2

National Council of Teachers of English (NCTE) for "'What Do You Really Care about Here?': Portfolios as Rites of Passage" by Judith Fueyo. From *Language Arts,* vol. 71, no. 6, October 1994, pp. 404–10. Reprinted with permission. All rights reserved.

Teaching K–8 for "User-Friendly Portfolios: The Search Goes On" by Susan Mandel Glazer, Katrin-Kaja Rooman, and Kristine Luberto. From *Teaching K–8,* November/December 1994, pp. 105–6. Reprinted with permission. All rights reserved.

Association for Supervision and Curriculum Development (ASCD) for "What Makes a Portfolio a Portfolio?" by F. Leon Paulson, Pearl R. Paulson, and Carol A. Meyer. From *Educational Leadership,* vol. 48, no. 5, February 1991, pp. 60–63. Reprinted with permission. All rights reserved.

Association for Supervision and Curriculum Development (ASCD) for "Portfolio Assessment: Sampling Student Work" by Dennie Palmer Wolf. From *Educational Leadership,* vol. 46, no. 7, April 1989, pp. 35–39. Reprinted with permission. All rights reserved.

International Society for Technology in Education (ISTE) for "Electronic Portfolios—Some Pivotal Questions" by Christopher Moersch and Louis M. Fisher III. From *Learning and Leading with Technology,* vol. 23, no. 2, October 1995, pp. 10–15. Reprinted with permission. All rights reserved.

Helen C. Barrett and the International Society for Technology in Education (ISTE) for "Technology-Supported Assessment Portfolios" by Helen C. Barrett. From *The Computing Teacher,* vol. 21, no. 6, March 1994, pp. 9–12. (Updated by Helen C. Barrett, September 1995.) Reprinted with permission. All rights reserved.

SECTION 3

National Council of Teachers of English (NCTE) for "Portfolios and Self-Assessment" by Leslie Ballard. From *English Journal*, vol. 81, no. 2, February 1992, pp. 46–48. Reprinted with permission. All rights reserved.

American Alliance for Health, Physical Education, Recreation, and Dance for "Portfolio Assessment: Documenting Authentic Student Learning" by Vincent J. Melograno. From *Journal of Physical Education, Recreation, and Dance*, vol. 65, no. 8, October 1994, pp. 50–55, 58–61. Reprinted with permission. All rights reserved.

F. Leon Paulson and Pearl R. Paulson for "Student-Led Portfolio Conferences" by F. Leon Paulson and Pearl R. Paulson, August 1994. Reprinted with permission. All rights reserved.

Vermont State Department of Education for "Portfolios and Your Child: Some Questions and Answers for Parents and Families," 1994. Reprinted with permission. All rights reserved.

Association for Supervision and Curriculum Development (ASCD) for "Portfolios Invite Reflection—from Students *and* Staff" by Elizabeth A. Hebert. From *Educational Leadership*, vol. 49, no. 8, May 1992, pp. 58–61. Reprinted with permission. All rights reserved.

Index

Learn from Our Books *and* from Our Authors!

Bring Our Author/Trainers to Your District

At IRI/Skylight, we have assembled a unique team of outstanding author/trainers with international reputations for quality work. Each has designed high-impact programs that translate powerful new research into successful learning strategies for every student. We design each program to fit your school's or district's special needs.

Training Programs

Gain practical techniques and strategies for implementing the latest findings from educational research. IRI/Skylight is recognized around the world for its commitment to translating cognitive and cooperative learning research into high-quality resource materials and effective classroom practices. In each program IRI/Skylight designs, participants learn by doing the thinking and cooperating they will be asking their students to do. With IRI/Skylight's specially prepared materials, participants learn how to teach their students to learn for a lifetime.

Networks for Systemic Change

Through partnerships with Phi Delta Kappa and others, IRI offers two Networks for site-based systemic change: *The Network of Mindful Schools* and *The Multiple Intelligences School Network.* The Networks are designed to promote systemic school change as practical and possible when starting with a renewed vision that centers on *what* and *how* each student learns.

Training of Trainers

The Training of Trainers programs train your best teachers, those who provide the highest quality instruction, to coach other teachers. This not only increases the number of teachers you can afford to train in each program, but also increases the amount of coaching and follow-up that each teacher can receive from a resident expert. Our Training of Trainers programs will help you make a systemic improvement in your staff development program.

To receive a free copy of the IRI/Skylight catalog, find out more about the Networks for Systemic Change, or receive more information about trainings offered through IRI/Skylight, contact

IRI/Skylight Training and Publishing, Inc.
200 E. Wood St., Suite 274, Palatine, IL 60067
800-348-4474
FAX 847-991-6420

There are

one-story intellects,

two-story intellects, and three-story

intellects with skylights. All fact collectors, who have

no aim beyond their facts, are one-story men. Two-story men compare,

reason, generalize, using the labors of the fact collectors as well as their

own. Three-story men idealize, imagine, predict—

their best illumination comes from

above, through the skylight.

—*Oliver Wendell*

Holmes

(IRI) SkyLight

TRAINING AND PUBLISHING, INC.